POST-OAK CIRCUIT.

BY

A MEMBER OF THE RED RIVER CONFERENCE.

"Ephraim feedeth on wind."—Hos. xii. 1.
"As poor, yet making many rich."—2 Cor. vi. 10.

EDITED BY THOS. O. SUMMERS, D.D.

Nashville, Tenn.:
PUBLISHED FOR THE AUTHOR,
BY E. STEVENSON & F. A. OWEN.
1857.

STEREOTYPED AND PRINTED BY A. A. STITT,
SOUTHERN METHODIST PUBLISHING HOUSE, NASHVILLE, TENN

TO THE PEOPLE CALLED

METHODISTS:

TO THE JONATHAN THAT IS IN THEM:

This Volume

IS

RESPECTFULLY INSCRIBED.

Contents.

Introduction.

On looking at the title-page of this book, the reader will probably ask, "Who is this member of the Red River Conference? and where is that Conference—in the Northern or Southern division of the Methodist Church?" We are not at liberty to answer these questions. All we are empowered to say is, "Post-Oak Circuit" has an author—why he does not divulge his name, he has not condescended to inform us. Were we to publish it, it might secure an extended circulation of his book, in both the North and South, and especially in the South-west; but this we may not do; and so the book must win its way to public favor, if it can, by its own intrinsic merits. That it will do this, the reader will scarcely doubt.

We have several essays on the support of the

ministry and kindred topics—and good ones too—but "Post-Oak Circuit" is *sui generis*—there is nothing like it in all our literature. Unless we are mistaken, old Avarice himself will read it with interest, shut it up, wipe his eyes, and—open his purse!

If any who read this book should think they have been sitting for certain portraits which they will find in it, we have only to say that while the artist appears to have found his characters in real life, and to have drawn them to the life, we are not aware that there is a single personal allusion in the whole volume; and those who think they have found their likenesses in it had better keep the discovery to themselves as far as they can, and profit by it as much as they may.

We have only to add that the author, according to his accustomed liberality, intends devoting the profits of the sale of his book to a pious and charitable purpose, which in due time will be made public.

The Editor.

NASHVILLE, TENN., March 23, 1857.

Preface.

A LARGE amount of property, in the shape of lands, crops, flocks, herds, houses, machinery, manufactured goods, bills of exchange, and specie, is held by certain individuals of this country, who profess themselves to be the "stewards of the Lord"—believing it a duty to profess even the figments of the faith. Of the yield of all these fields, the Lord receives a very small pittance. As their owner he is practically ignored. He appears in them only as a gleaner, where seldom fall the partial handfuls of a kinsman. One may reckon up individual Methodists in almost any county who make annually for themselves more money than the whole fifteen hundred thousand in all the States pay to the cause of missions.

Jonathan has learned to turn a handsome penny at professing religion. He promptly recognizes as valid any claim of Christian benevolence upon him which you may present; but directly he insists that you shall take it out in hearing him sing or tell his experience; and if the claim is a very heavy one or very pressing, he can talk like a saint or sing like a whitehead. Verily the children of *this* generation are as wise in their day as the children of any generation.

Our friend is likewise a great believer in the economy of a millennium: he luxuriates in its prospect, and gloriously rests in the promises. Confident that "the day when all shall know the Lord" will come—that the time is set, and the Church is well backed by prophecy—he thinks that, do or not do, the coming of the kingdom car neither be much helped nor hindered; though do not understand him to be a Calvinist: sooner than that, he will give something.

Contemplating his particular case as instrumentally connected with the conversion of a world, one is compelled to an increased reliance upon the naked force of prophecy.

Methodism breaks down under its own weight. Our people spend nothing for jewelry or fine dress; do n't go to the opera or balls; give small salaries to their preachers; give moderately to the heathen; and are as industrious as beavers. Therefore the eyes of our Church stand out with fatness: she has more than heart can wish. She is at once—we say it humbly—the richest, the most covetous, and the most orthodox Church extant. She can say, without exaggerating, "I am rich, and increased with goods, and have need of nothing."

We are as well satisfied with Mr. Wesley's liberality ("our great founder," by the by) as if it were our own. Mr. Wesley's poverty, at death, is a peculiarly gratifying fact. He yet lives in history, the remains of a great civilization. We look at him as a child would at an antediluvian fossil ninety feet long. Long may our Church flourish on the reminiscences of ancestral fame!

BREAKING THE ICE—HORTATORY.

To Seven Members of the Methodist Church:*

Dear Brethren:—You have been appointed, officially, to raise the wind: in the language of the magnificent East, to bring the wind out of your treasuries. The wind brought quails from the sea; and among quartermasters the four winds are the greatest. "Awake, O North wind; and come, thou South: blow upon my garden, that the spices thereof may flow out."

You have done wisely: you have sown the wind; for "whatsoever a man soweth, that shall he also reap." Ephraim fed on

---

* Why name my melancholy friends?

wind, and filled his belly with the east wind; though, as is evident, he objected not to corn; for "Ephraim loveth to tread out the corn." Hosea x. 11.

If at all descended from Ephraim, I am of that part of him which loved corn; not of that which ate wind. In this, I trust, I am not earthly, for "He gave them of the corn of heaven, and man did eat angels' food." Ps. lxxviii. 24. Indeed, good angels delight in substance; and when Abraham spread them a table under the oak in Mamre, they ate of butter, meal-cakes, a roast, and milk—solid food, such as they who would fain entertain angels unawares had as well set before strangers.

My dear brethren, have a care lest you raise too little corn. O, I wish that each of you were a Joseph in Egypt, with the key of a thousand corn-cribs hanging at his girdle! I remain, as ever, your friend,

THE AUTHOR.

POST-OAK CIRCUIT.

CHAPTER I.

"OLD SHIP OF ZION"—FARE GREATLY REDUCED.

"A THING is worth what it costs." This rule would determine the value of a name and a place in the household of faith, and refutes the notion that infinites cannot be estimated. Doubtless many a reader *can* count the actual cost of the gospel to him, reckoning for the whole period from the first day that he was translated from darkness to this present one inclusive. In such a calculation, it would be well to throw out fractions. During the Levitical dispensation, this estimate could have been more readily made, as the cost then consisted in whole articles, say a sheep or a bullock, or so many bushels of grain, or hins of oil; which amounted every year to one sheep for every five that a man had, or one peck for every bushel. Though tithes are no longer brought into the sanctuary in *kind*, it would be well to reckon their amount in that way. The problem would then be, How many beeves have you paid into the Lord's treasury since you were converted? How many mules?*

---

* During a recent missionary excitement in Alabama, a Baptist brother became sufficiently alive to his duty to give one hundred dollars ($100) to the cause at a Methodist meeting. His friends became alarmed, waited upon him, and protested that in so much excitement he was not rightly at himself. "Well, my friends," replied he, "I lost a mule the other day worth $120, and none of you came to sympathize with me; and now, that I have given $100 to carry the gospel to

It must be admitted that the cost of salvation has been greatly cheapened since the days of the first tabernacle. In this, at least, we have had "progress." The prophet's call, "Ho, every one! come ye, buy wine and milk without money and without price!" is now nearly fulfilled; and his bounty is pretty much accepted upon his own terms. The old quarter-dollar quarterage story—alas! too old—has done good service to the—certainly not to the Church. It has been used in the main to glorify "the Old Ship," at the expense of other Churches which charge a higher rate of fare, though not very high. A large part of the Western ministry have paid the penalty of that quarter-dollar anecdote, without knowing what they were paying for. It presented

---

the heathen, you think I am crazy!" The circuit-preacher told the fact all around the circuit; and the answer of the generous Baptist yielded the missionary treasury many an additional dollar.

the Methodist Church and ministry in a false light, and brought down the membership to a fatal economy. It was a great mistake to say that Methodist preaching costs nothing, or even to think it. It costs a living in all cases. If the people do not pay it, the preacher does. If one man escapes paying his share of the cost, his neighbor pays it for him: if one neighborhood, it is at the expense of another. The cost is often shifted, but never escaped. It is the glory of the Methodist Church that she has reduced this cost to a *minimum.** Here

---

* Various reasons have been assigned by different persons as the cause of this reduced state of things: that it is because an *itinerant* ministry is not so favorable to endearing ties as a settled; that it is the result of an overcare of the people for the spiritual welfare of their preachers; (lest they become "full, and say, Who is the Lord?") other some, that the primary injunction, "No scrip, no money, in *their* purse," has not been corrected for the present times, and is therefore quietly understood by the people as being still of force. Of these, the first-named reason is the least

she has led the way. From the first, she unfurled this banner. It waves brightly over her wealthy plains. It floats from her steepled churches. It rallies with its ethereal motto her anxious stewards. It is inscribed on the hearts of her people: "PRAY YOUR WAY."

The Methodist Church has doubtless had the "candle" which giveth "light to all that are in the house;" but she has also had the "bushel." A philosophy of her history

---

satisfactory. A few years since, an Episcopal minister, settled in O., Louisiana, was called by the force of controlling circumstances to sever those "endearing ties." Such occasions are always affecting, and usually well attended. The minister's farewell sermon—who has not heard it with sad interest? Towards the conclusion of his discourse, the reverend gentleman (Mr. B.) looked over his audience, and remarked:—If there was any one in the house who could prove that he had ever given one dollar towards *his* support, it should be refunded on the spot. The Methodists are not easily excelled when they set themselves to do a thing, but in this instance they must yield the unwilling palm, for a *minimum* is surpassed by the *reductio ad nil.*

might be aptly entitled, "The Bushel *versus* The Candle."

It has been no slight conflict. The bushel is not an outright extinguisher, for a candle can burn under it: the main difficulty is, that the light then benefits no one, not even the lighter. A vessel for measuring grain may be understood to signify wealth; and a bushel—the largest that is used—may justly enough represent the wealth of the Methodist Church.

As the General Conference has ordered some one to design a uniform Church-seal, it is respectfully suggested that it be—A bushel, bottom up, (the candle supposed tc be under,) with the motto,

"*Longe ora:*
Minime da."

CHAPTER II.

THE GOSPEL ON TICK.

THE precious gospel costs some very little, yet there are others who pay less. These are not more honorable than those, only more fortunate. Convinced that wisdom is not to be mentioned with pearls or rubies, they are careful not to do it. An allusion to the gold of Ophir in connection with the "wisdom divine" thrills their whole man: they have been known to go out of the church with the sound in their ears; or else to remain composed, if possible, with closed eyes, during the entire process of "lifting the collection," scarcely conscious of the approach of the faithful steward with the black bag. O how grateful they feel. How completely they realize man's inadequacy to repay "one of a thousand!" Infinite charity! Freely they have received: freely they—sing. Behold the fowls of the air, and all the preachers, which have neither storehouse nor barn; yet are they all fed! Mysterious providence! Others have come forward, and have paid the minister ere *they* were aware. And so the good man has gone to another field freighted with their gratitude and their blessing. Such a development of "*by faith only*" must be the crowning glory of any Protestant church; and such members are the jewels of our mother. How they give forth the rays of their light, against the background of a world wholly given up to the main chance! These keep far away from our fold those shepherds who seek only the fleece: they guarantee for ever a self-denying ministry. Never could the reader doubt the measure which this joint supplieth, had he known Brother Jeremiah Larkum.

"Brother Jerry," as they called him, often said in his experience, that he was brought down under the song of the "Old Family Bible—that lay on the stand." The reflection that it still lay there always seemed to overpower him. When he came to that part, almost everybody felt for him, except the stewards, who did nothing but groan. Brother Jerry rather warmed under it, and "had great liberty." He usually wound up by singing,

> "I want to be as happy
> As I well can be," etc.;

or held his handkerchief to his mouth and twisted down on his seat, smothering a shout. He used to bring it in that he was thankful for "a full promise and a free gospel:" that he always rejoiced in its "light-as-a-feather burdens," and its "easy-pulling yokes." He warned young professors against "cross-shirking." "Many," said he, "look at the cross a long ways off; others walk round it; some touch it with their littlest finger; once in a while somebody takes it up; but my advice to you all is, POCKET IT!" He was striving for that distant land, and sometimes thought he could see its "milk-and-honey branches" from his "Pisgah-closet:" that if he met with no "gospel-mishap"—and he thought he should not—he was "bound to get there."

Old Brother Goodsine, the recording steward of "Post-Oak Circuit," used to say that Brother Jerry was a good *spirit-gauge:* if he spoke among the first, the meeting was most sure to be a drag; if in the middle, it was so-so; but if he held off until it was over, there was most always a good time.

John Bear, another of the stewards, an honest, noble-looking fellow, who usually hit the centre—being, as it happened, a gunsmith—used to say that Jerry was "all talk and no cider." When Jerry's license to exhort was to be renewed, the majority said he was "very feeling sometimes," and they did not think that he "could do much harm no ways." But John Bear was, as he said, "up and down against it:" for his part, Jerry might talk till doomsday, and it would not turn the color of a hair, unless he paid his church-subscription last year, and the year before, and every other year. "Let him pay down and prove up!" said he, striking his open palm with his fist: "pay down his cash and prove up his faith!" That Brother Jerry went to glory too soon anyhow; according to his mind, he always went off half-cocked, so he doubted whether he got there more than one time in ten. "No, no," he added, "when Jerry groans less and gives more, he may get my vote, but not before."

It was agreed that the elder should give Brother Larkum a talk: and then it was agreed that Brother Jerry was a hard case anyhow.

Brother Jerry was wont to say that he had never met the man yet that could tell him the difference between exhorting and preaching; nor one that could show where one left off and the other began. One day the congregation at Oakville were all waiting, but the circuit-preacher did not come. Jerry was soon up in the pulpit. The parson, he said, had thrown all of them into a grief, and himself into a great quandary; but he looked to their "fellow-feelings" to help him on with this "big cross all-in-a-tremble." He gave out that his "*motto*" lay in the fifth chapter of the Song of Solomon, "in the bosom of the first verse: '*I have eaten my honey-comb with my honey.*' And now, friends," said he, "I may buzz about a little at first, by way of getting off; but you see how it is: I come to you on the wing, on the scared-up wing of a providentially-called-for exhortation. And my desire is, as soon as I naturally can, to take you in a bee-line to a gospel-gum. My motto is a regular bee-gum, the onliest tree in all the woods. Now, I ask, why is the gospel honey? and again I ask, why is honey the gospel? And I answer, *firstly*, because it is good for the hungry. And, *secondly*, I answer, because it is cheap. And now again, firstly, it is good for the hungry. The Scriptures say, 'To the hungry soul every bitter thing is sweet;' how sweet, then, must sweetening itself be! When a man is hungry, he is not particular: he will eat a good deal of comb to get some honey. A great many sermonizing sermons are curious-made and have a clear beauty, like white comb in which the bees have not yet put honey. Even *that* a man might eat." He had, he said, in his time, eaten a great deal of trash to get a little pure gospel—his honey-comb with his honey—and he felt all the better for it. For his part, he never found fault with what he got when he robbed a gum; he never had the heart to look a gift-horse in the mouth, though he felt himself as good a judge of a horse as any one, excepting it might be the elder. If it was generally most a poor preach, it was likewise most generally poor pay. These had been joined together, and he would not dare to give them a Moses's-bill of divorcement.

But also, *secondly*, it was cheap. It was wild honey; the wayfaring man could get it. If it was not cheap, it would not be gospel-honey—"without money, without price." But it *was* cheap. "You ask what is the strength of the gospel? I answer, its strength lies in its cheapness; its cheapness is its strength. It is naturally as cheap as nature. You paid nothing: I paid nothing: we all paid nothing: everybody paid nothing. Yet we have it, I have it, you have it. I heard old Sister Hardiman say, that when she and her husband first came to these parts, he saw a young man, one Sunday, standing back in the church, crying, while the minister was opening the doors. 'Young man,' said Brother Hardiman, 'why not go up and join?' 'I want to,' says he, 'but they tell me I must pay the preacher a barrel of corn first, and I have n't got it.' Now, friends, could you think that ever anybody thought that it cost anybody any thing to be a Methodist? Where in reason, in science, and in history, could that young man have been ever since he was born? In my whole life in the old North State, and some years out of her, never did I hear of such out-of-the-way Scripture-ignorance. Now, there is the West India long-sweetning and the West India short-sweetning; both of them sweet, but not cheap. But honey is both sweet and cheap: just like the gospel. The gospel, friends, that takes us to heaven, is cheap; and heaven, after we get there,

O how cheap and sweet! O, when I look out from my Pisgah-closet, I sometimes see a golden pear-shaped vision——." Here Jerry went off, and carried three of the congregation with him, till he came to

"I want to be as happy
As I well can be."

There he very easily made a stop.

As they all left the church, one of Jerry's admirers asked old Brother Goodsine what he thought of Brother Jerry's talk.

"Well," said the old man, "Brother Jerry is *some gum.*"

"Yes, he is," added John Bear; "but it's gum-log, not bee-gum."

"But, Father Goodsine," persisted the inquirer, "don't you think it was a right strong talk?"

"Nothing could be stronger," replied the old man, "on the subject of a cheap gospel than Brother Jerry's talk, unless it is Brother Jerry's example."

"As to Brother Jerry's cheap gospel," said John Bear, "being an exhorter has made a great change in Brother Jerry; for fifteen years he has had the gospel on tick, but now he is a tick on the gospel."

CHAPTER III.

SMALL POTATOES—"THE WIDOW'S MITE."

NOTHING can transcend the ingenuity of man, except it is the ingenuity of a church-steward. The problem is to collect money for the support of the gospel, and wonderful is the solution. He levies contribution upon all things animate that may come within reach of his bag on a Sunday; and on week-days he spreads his plans, like fresh spider's webs, to catch small current particles, which otherwise might be still floating and invisible, except in sunbeams. Occasionally he secures a resisting sinner, extracts from him his mite—that is, bleeds him—and then hangs him up in his calculations, as a dead fly, for the rest of the season. He does not despise the day of small things, else he would despise every day in the year. The world is to be subdued; but a subdued world is to him a very distant world; and therefore, as he has it in his eye, it is a very small world. He says, if every man, and every woman, and every young person, and every child, would each do their duty, it would not require much: five cents here and five cents there soon count up.

Some years since, it was discovered that the world could be converted, in good time, at the moderate cost of a cent a week to each Church-member.* O, how it sprang the Church and thrilled the stewards! Nothing had been in the way worth minding

* A cent a week for the cause of missions was actually proposed and advocated by the Missionary Board of the Methodist Church, several years ago, as the quota of a Church-member! This would not have exceeded one-hundredth of one per cent. upon the wealth of the membership.

but the expense: now *that* was removed, and Zion was ready to travail. Most every one had felt that faith and prayer were great means in most cases; but in regard to converting the heathen these means presented a painful process, requiring to their efficiency a corresponding money appropriation which it was appalling to contemplate. Paralyzed with estimates that threatened the Church of the New Testament with the burdens of the Church in Egypt, when the way of escape was made plain, by the happy thought of cheapening the actual cost of furnishing the gospel to the world, and not by increasing the tax upon the membership, it was like laying the corner-stone of the Millennium. Old class-leaders and stewards, exhorters, preachers, and people, "wept with a loud voice, and many shouted aloud for joy, so that the people could not discern the noise of the shout of joy from the noise of the weeping of the people; for the people shouted with a loud shout, and the noise was heard afar off." When the scheme of the Mission Board first came out in the New York "Advocate," Brother Bunting Badger, a hearty Englishman of fifty-six years of age, and a Wesleyan, who had been in this country some twenty years, and a steward of the Post-Oak Circuit for the last ten, actually spent the greater part of one day in his own shop, shaking hands and talking over the "'Appy haction that 'ad coome down by the last post." He assured Brothers Jacob Oakhart and Squire Wallet, both of them circuit officials, that it was "the very thing, the very thing: a flash, do ye see! from over the Atlantic."

Brother Oakhart was an exhorter, who had been licensed mainly in view of the blacks, for whose edification he seemed to be constitutionally and religiously gifted. Though his speech was not with enticing words of man's wisdom, he was curiously eloquent within the comprehension of his responsive audience. "Massa Oakhart was on his high hoss, he really was dis day," said Uncle Clay. "He piled hisself on hisself. He made the cold chills run over and over me. The hair of my head snapped like frost. I speaks de raal truf." Though scarcely turned of fifty, Clay had a remarkably bushy head of gray hair; and as all negroes prefer being as near one hundred years old as possible, he was fond of alluding to "the hair of my head." This fine organ was the basis of no little pomp and considerable position, it being the only appreciable superiority its owner had over several brethren of his own color and of equal standing.

Squire Wallet was the wealthiest member in the circuit, and was elected steward pretty much in view of that fact. It was thought that the old fellow could occasionally, perhaps, be rung in to the tune of the Last Quarter. The last Quarterly Conference is rather a pressing time, when the financial child of the year comes to the birth, and there is often not strength to bring forth. It was thought that the squire, having a hundred and twenty hands, could be stirred at that travailing moment to do something. But the squire was never to be caught but once. The agony of that hour, and an extra ten dollars, taught him a lesson which he never forgot. He was always anxious afterward to be present at the last quarterly meeting in the year, but his memory "never served him fair." "O," he would add, looking up, "how uncertain are all our calculations this side of eternity! Yes, yes, Brother Badger, our days *are* as a post: it *is* an overwhelming thought," said the squire.

"I say," said the Englishman, "that every American and English mind should adopt the immortal expression of the great Bunting—do ye see!—'Repentance, faith, holiness, a penny a week and a shilling a quarter

How full, and yet how simple—do ye see! There it is, the soul and the body of Christianity. Every man is rich enough to do that: it is not much—do ye see!"

"No, Brother Badger, no; there is none of us rich enough to do any thing, nor will be till we are in our graves. The grave, the grave only is rich. If I had what's in the grave, then I grant you I should be rich. Only give me all the niggers that's been buried in there, and then you might call me rich. O!" said he, looking up,

"'Their names are graven on the stone,
Their bones are in the clay.'"

The pleasure which Brother Badger, the Squire, and Jacob Oakhart found in talking to each other was peculiar, yet not uncommon. It lay in neither listening to the other, excepting only long enough to catch a suggestive word, from which one might start in his own direction. Sometimes they were all three in ideas; if so, they all talked to each other promiscuously at once; but usually, while one was running off a train of thought, the other two were firing up two other trains.

"Yes—do ye see!" said Badger, "the gospel is no longer a hexperiment; the 'eathen can now 'ave it on the very heasiest terms by this haction; the very heasiest to ourselves and to them; the very thing for *both*—do ye see!"

"We may well talk about the heathen," said Jacob Oakhart: "they will soon be in their graves. We count them like bugs, by the million, and value them by quarters and dimes. But, mind, as I tell my colored brethren, those very same heathen will string us millstone necklaces out of our small change, and sink us among great black waves, the swell of five hundred storms of wrath, which will dash a wrecked man and search for him over the spot where he goes down."

"The heathen," said Squire Wallet, "are

fond of ornaments; they dance to the sounds of martial and festival music, and jingle their necklaces of lump-gold." He continued, with an imposing air, "Give me the gold, and the silver, and the pearls, and the diamonds, in the shields and spears, in the bracelets and rings, which have been put down into the grave with those heathen, and I would give you my home-farm, I would, and say thanky' to it too! Yes, you give *me* the Catacombs, the Pyramids, and the kings in them, just as they were buried, and *you* take the farm all the time. O!" he exclaimed,

"'The grave! how deserted and drear!
 With the noise of the wild wind,
The creaks of the bier,
 And the white bones all clattering together!'"

"The best *bones* I ever had," said Oakhart, "was on the heathen. I there put in a colter on the minds of the colored members, that all ought to give to send the Bible to the heathen; not so many dimes or dollars, but so many skulls-full of money; that I had a mind to open an Indian mound and get two grown skulls for money-boxes; so when we took up a missionary-collection, and passed them round, the sight of the dead might rack the consciences of the living; that every black man ought to give a skull-full and every white man a grave-full of silver, or as nigh full as they could, in this world, if they wanted to be easy in the other. I told them I had a mind to get from the secretary a Chinaman's skull, a Fejee skull, a Guinea's skull, and a skull from Kamtschatka, and hang them up on pegs for collection-boxes; that when I took a collection for each kind of heathen, I should like to see the wretch of a Church-member that would divide one dime among all those skulls."

"Ye know, Squire," said Badger, "the Lord don't require much, if ye'll only do it.

'What doth the Lord ask but to do justly to love mercy, to walk humbly?' And that's easy—do ye see! easy all round, if every man will do his part; and ye know Hengland expects every man to do that, as the immortal Nelson said at the great Trafalgar. There would be enough left still for all of us, and the heathen and the preachers be as fat as Durhams besides. Only give me the spot, says Archimedes; and, do ye see! that the great Bunting has done: 'A penny a week and a shilling a quarter,' says he. And it's not much; you might do it and never know it. And yet, do ye see! it's a great deal; all added, I say, it's a great deal. 'Many a little mak's a muckle,' says Sawney; and he's right for once. Every man's shoulder to the wheel, and we need not cry to Hercules at all. Ye know that the widow's mite is all that the Lord asks; and that Brother Oakhart here can do as well as ye yourself, Squire. Why, man, it's the millennial dawn; every ha'penny is a beam of the latter day; every widow's mite is a pure beam; and all added together, do ye see! it's the Phœbus of the new heavens in his glittering chariot. Do ye not say so, Brother Goodsine?"

The old man had come into the store a moment before, and stood listening.

"Well," replied he, in a measured way, "in part I do. Ha'pennies and widow's mites, from men as rich as you and the Squire here, if you put enough of them together, might at least be considered the moonshine of the dust of the wheels of the glittering chariot of the millennial Phœbus."

Brother Badger was under such headway, the answer was lost. He kept on: "A cup of cold water, do ye see! shall not lose its reward: a merciful arrangement to him that gives and him that takes. It doesn't cost, and it does count. What is cheaper than water? and, do ye see! what charity so pure and beautiful? It's not the value—no, not the value. What! as the prophet says, 'Will the Lord be pleased with tnousands of rams or with ten thousands of rivers of oil?' No, no; it's mercy, it's the widow's mite, it's the cup of water, the penny and the shilling, the Lord wants; nothing less, and nothing more."

"*You* say," interposed Squire Wallet, "that Archimedes was strong: *I* say he was weak. Except the grave, nothing is strong. I should like to see him or anybody rig a purchase over the grave of one of my dead niggers, and *prize* him out. There's a chance for his lever! By the cholera, in three days, I lost thirty hands. 'O, rapacious, voracious, tenacious grave!' But *you* say, give him a fulcrum. So *I* say: give him *all* the grave-stones, everywhere, big and little—a pyramid of grave-stones. Then let him or anybody try himself on my patch of graves out there behind the quarters. I should be mighty glad to do it on shares, for half of all he'd raise, and thanky' too. But *I* know he couldn't do a thing: I wish he could. No, nothing grips tighter than the grave, or holds stronger. Archimedes himself could not try to do a harder thing than that; could he, Father Goodsine?"

"No, Squire, no, I think not," said the old man; "unless it might be, to get a little quarterage out of some of our Church-members."

CHAPTER IV.

"LORD, WHAT A WRETCHED LAND IS THIS,
THAT YIELDS US NO SUPPLY!"—*Hymn.*

ONE of the greatest phenomena of ecclesiastical finance is that of the female membership of a wealthy church turned into a sewing-machine. It is easily identified, by some half-dozen carriages standing about the parsonage, or the humble abode of some poor sister, for two hours or so, periodically. It forms a season of delightful leisure and reünion to the drivers, footboys, and waiting-women, who come to wait on their mistresses, and see them work. It is an hour, too, of good things, of cakes, of curiosity, of week-day and Sunday news; a time of admiration, of exclamation, of calculation, as well as of downright hard sewing. Such a gathering certainly presents one of the most interesting of studies to a mind at all curious as to the number and variety of forms into which Christian benevolence is capable of crystallizing.

It would seem that money got in any common way was not good enough to be used for the purposes of our holy religion. It must be wrung out of one by some unusual method. It must come harder than any other money—which, in fact, it does—or else it will not seem to answer the purpose. Ladies will work half a day for half a dollar, on a sewing-society shirt, and feel that they have done a good work; when, in fact, to have put their hand in a purse, and given that sum, would only have been to save it from the next candy-shop. But they cannot bring themselves to believe that candy-money is the same as church-money. The largest dollar current is the church-dollar. It has an effect upon the optic nerve that has never yet been satisfactorily explained. The illusion, when the eye dwells on it a few moments, is that it grows.* Whether this is an illusion merely or not, it is certain that persons who would scarcely be conscious of the expenditure of ten, fifty, or a hundred dollars, in buying trinkets for their daughters, or in the general waste of a profuse

---

* A similar illusion occurred in the case of an Irish singing-master. Soon after arriving in this country he opened a singing-school. He set his terms at what seemed to him a high rate—a dollar for twelve lessons—and waited the result. He was agreeably surprised to find quite a number of pupils at the appointed hour, and that one had brought the tuition fee in advance—a silver dollar. The lesson commenced. "Wall," said the master aside, feeling the dollar in his pocket, "that is a large pace! Now, then, [aloud,] let's have it once more: sound all togither. Wall, [aside,] that is a *large* dollar! Now, mark ye, [aloud,] when B is flat, mi is in E. Wall, wall, [aside, taking out the dollar, and looking at it,] the very largest dollar I *iver* saw is that dollar!"

family, or in the purchase of fancy stock, or in agricultural experiments, or in the advancing some political interest, have been known to suffer great and continued depression on parting with a like sum for the support of the gospel. The entire amount collected annually by the Methodist Church in the whole United States, North and South, for the cause of missions, is, say three hundred and fifty thousand dollars; which seems a great deal—a very great deal—*of that sort of money.* But the United States spends in keeping up a single frigate about one thousand dollars a day, or three hundred and sixty-five thousand dollars annually; which, after all, does not seem so very much of *that* sort of money. "What wonders grace can do!" exclaim our people, as they contemplate those massive offerings of their poverty-stricken souls.

The church of the Post-Oak Circuit had in it a good deal of wealth; but, unfortunately, it existed, for the most part, still *in the ore*, which, it would seem, was only to be smelted by the furnace of Hinnom; for neither the tears of widows and orphans, nor the actual wants of their ministers, nor yet the fire of the Holy Ghost, had the effect of fusing it. Squire Wallet was its wealthiest member, but there were a dozen that worked from twenty to thirty hands each. All were good to the stewards for some trifle; but as they had been taught to do little, they learned to do less. Brother Badger was rather popular with the church as a steward. In the first place, as the society-treasurer, he gave credit for every mill contributed; and in the next place, he kept up the spirits of the membership, which were threatened more and more every year with a confirmed melancholy at the thought of having to support the preacher. He was for ever devising financial cobwebs to catch motes: "Many hands make light work;

and it 's not much if ye 'll all do a little; and the women as well as the men. Ye can make garments, like Dorcas; and many is the cent ye can get for them. Every cent and every stitch that ye give is a beam of the coming day; and all the beams gathered up make the big sun, do ye see!"

And so there was a regular sewing-society at work at old Sister Hardiman's every Wednesday. Sister Wallet had brought a large lot of negro clothing, a job for the society. The Squire had got thrown back by sickness on his place, and concluded to have his clothing made out. He was in a hurry to have it made up, the society agreed to do it at a very low rate, and so the job was secured. Brother Badger looked in, and assured them that "Hit was one of those mysterious hopenings of that Providence that supplies the fowls of the hair with food."

"Only," replied one of the ladies, "they neither sow nor reap; but as for us, it 's true we don't reap much, but we *sew* a great deal."

"O, ye 've a talent, all of ye, to improve, and I am glad ye have—stitch to stitch, talent to talent—to be true to a little, that's the gospel secret," rejoined the treasurer, as he shut the door, and retired.

"If Brother Badger would spend more of *his* talents, he would know more of the secret of the Lord," said Sister Hardiman. "My sight," continued she, "is now too dim to help much, but in my day I have done my share of work, perhaps, in getting up fairs, and in sewing-societies, strawberry parties, parsonage suppers, and other make-shifts* of the stewards. But I am free to

---

* "Why not throttle old avarice or whatever else stands in the way of cheerful giving—throttle and kill him by honest and direct blows? These shifts are miserable. Is the pill of doing good so bitter that it must be sugar-coated or disguised, that one may take it without knowing it?

"We have actually known people go to more outlay of

say that, excepting in a very few instances, I have thought the whole thing unnecessary, if not hurtful to the society. It is a poor remedy for stinginess in a church : it rather aggravates the disease. To give directly largely to the support of the gospel is a New Testament obligation which must be impressed upon every church until it is felt. All indirect methods of raising money for this purpose ought to be promptly rejected. By such methods the money just then needed may possibly be had, but every dollar got costs ten in the notion which it creates and confirms, of supposing ourselves not actually required to *give* to the Lord. The least 'value received' at fairs, in pen-wipers, or

---

money and money's worth, to say nothing of pains-taking, to get up a fair for roofing a shed, or furnishing a parsonage, or paying a church-debt, than would have footed the bill by a plain subscription. Where human nature has to be coaxed along so, and led blindfold to storming the redoubts of selfishness, grace has much work yet to do."—*New Orleans Christian Advocate.*

at suppers, in the shape of frozen cream or in a syllabub, changes the complexion of the whole transaction: it ceases to yield the conscious reward of an act of Christian benevolence."*

* An item, which appeared in a public print of recent date, is significant to those who have experienced benevolent suppers and Christian fairs. A very successful fair had just come off, at which "ten dollars" was asked by a young lady for a plate of "gumbo." The alarmed individual who had called for it put down fifty cents, and told her to choose between the half-dollar and the gumbo. Another ate a slice of turkey, and then learned that it was "two dollars;" which he paid, and left. That one gobbler yielded the church over a hundred dollars—a larger sum than the lifetime-contribution of many a member—despite the motto that "a living dog is better than a dead lion." Hence the tone of the public stomach needed to be restored by the following rate of prices, which "was published," (says the editor,) "at the request of the ladies, for the benefit of the charitable community."

"*Scale of Prices established by the Committee of Arrangements.*—Supper of meats, fifty cents; supper of meats, with chicken salad, seventy-five cents; gumbo, per plate, twenty-five cents; coffee, per cup, ten cents; chocolate, per cup, ten cents; lemonade, per glass, ten cents; ice-cream, with cake, twenty-five cents; ice-

"Well, Grandma," said one of the ladies, "then I understand you not to approve of this sewing-society."

"In its principle, my dear child, I certainly do not. I always give way in such things to others, and help them on cheerfully, but I hope yet to live to see a better groundwork of duty wrought into our loved Methodism, in supporting its ministry and its missions. The plan of collecting moneys for the missionary society by selling life-memberships has lost, I fear, thousands of dollars to the cause of missions. It has substituted one motive for another—the motive of complimenting our friends for the sublime one of sending the gospel to the world. It places

---

cream, with cake and fruit, thirty cents; sherbets, per glass, twenty-five cents; jellies, per glass, twenty-five cents; Charlotte-russe, twenty-five cents; fruit-cake, per slice, twenty cents; pound-cake, per slice, fifteen cents; sponge-cake, per slice, fifteen cents; macaroons, etc., four for ten cents; soda, per glass, ten cents. Change given in all cases."

the claims of the heathen equivocally before the Church, instead of a clear announcement of the great truth that it is her awful duty to supply life to dying myriads."

"But, Grandma," said another sister, "by fairs, sewing-societies, and so on, there 's many a cent saved out of the fire, which otherwise would only be wasted; and still, those who wish to give larger amounts have a chance to do it."

"I doubt," replied the old lady, "if by such artificial excitants to duty, we do not lose more by the fire than we save out of it. Whatever susceptibility I might once have had to all plans for procuring means to support and spread the doctrines of Christ *without feeling it,* I have been thoroughly cured by my observation of Brother Badger and his penny-a-week schemes, his 'widows' mites,' and his solitary 'sunbeams.' Such mottoes might do for England, where the country is thickly settled. the territory small, and every man easily looked after; and I understand the great Bunting has achieved financial wonders among the Wesleyans; but I am sure he never did it by collecting only 'a penny a week and a shilling a quarter,' which would only be two dollars a year per member, a sum upon which the ministry could conveniently starve. He might have said it as a motto, but I'm sure he never used it as a measure."

"But, Grandma, a good many cannot give more than that in a year," said a sister.

"That's a very common mistake, my dear," responded the old lady, "a very great mistake. What! in this country, where nearly every man owns land and lives in plenty—where the common laborer earns an easy and abundant support for himself and family—to say that the earnings of one day in three hundred and sixty-five, at the rate of the pay of a day-laborer, is all that most people can give! Would that *we* had never heard of 'Doctor Bunting,' or the 'widow's mite,' as Brother Badger enforces them!

"For ten years he has sounded into his own ears and those of the members, that a little—only a little—is needed from each one, until he has come to believe, and the society with him, that it is really so; that ten dollars is enough for himself and others of the richest men in the circuit; that everybody else ought to do as much; that if the minister is not supported, the sin lies elsewhere than at their door: whereas, a hundred dollars a year to the ministry of the word and a hundred to missions, would scarcely secure him an easy conscience at a dying-hour; for in twenty years he has increased in wealth more than fifty thousand dollars. Brother Goodsine, with a large family and but two or three hands, has scarcely ever given less than one hundred dollars a year."

"You would not gauge everybody by old

Mr. Goodsine, I trust," exclaimed a lady; "you know that every one thinks Mr. Goodsine crazy on the subject of giving."

"I certainly would," answered the old lady. "If Brother Goodsine is crazy on any subject, I should like to become acquainted with the really sensible men!"

"O, not on any thing else, Grandma, for I admit there are few men as sensible as Mr. Goodsine," rejoined the lady.

"Well, my dear, believe me," continued the old lady, "Brother Goodsine is sensible to the last. It is not that he has less sense than others, but more religion. But I can cite you to others. There is Brother John Bear, who is poorer still: he never gives less than fifty dollars, and often nearer a hundred. Then there is Brother Oakhart."

"What!" exclaimed one of the young ladies, 'Heartoak?'"

"Yes, my dear. 'Heartoak,' as the boys call him, does more—gaunt as he looks, in his clean, bad-fitting, home-spun, copperas clothes — than any wealthy man in our church. He has his house hung round with missionary certificates, as he has a way of making each one of his children, as soon as they come into the world, a life-member of the parent society. Poor as he is, he manages to have the frame for the picture and the cash ready, waiting the arrival of the young life-member."

"Well, certainly," said they all, laughing, "Brother Oakhart *is* a curious man. And," added one, "what a curious preacher!"

"Yes; and *I* call him a very fine preacher, notwithstanding the words of his own manufacture," said the old lady. "He makes the truth plain and very impressive to everybody, especially to the blacks. I once heard him preach on the cause of missions, and shall never forget it. He said that missionary collections should always be lifted in the skulls of dead heathen. I have never put a dollar into the missionary plate since without asking myself, 'How much would you give were it the silent appeal of a pagan's skull?' It is true, Brother Oakhart sometimes steps from the sublime to the ridiculous, but much oftener from the ridiculous to the sublime. I wish there were more men full as curious, or, rather, that he was not so singular in his generosity. But, my dears, I 'm doing all the talking and finding all the fault: it is time for me to stop."

"You are doing all the praising, too, Grandma; you forget that."

"It 's very little praising that I can do, my child, when talking on the subject of the money-matters of the Methodist Church. The only really bitter moments I have, are those in which I dwell upon the privations and agonies which have been endured on this circuit by ministers and their families. I sometimes fear that I did not do *my* duty; that I might have done more to arouse the

6

church to its duty; or, if I could not extract the dart, I might at least have lessened the pang. You must not wonder at me if I talk with what may seem a morbid earnestness on this subject."

"Yes," said Sister Wallet, "we have had hard times on this circuit."

"True enough, my dear," returned the old lady; "it was not the circuit, however, that saw the hard times, but the poor preachers who happened to be sent to it."

"For years and years, you know," said an elderly sister, "Brother Cabot had the management of all the money-matters of the circuit, and we hardly knew whether the preacher was paid or not."

"Why so?" said a young lady; "was n't Brother Cabot honest?"

"O yes," replied the other, "he was honest; but then, you know, the membership usually give more or less, just as the principal steward interests himself for the preacher."

"What was his name—Cabot?" said the young lady: "I wonder if his family were at all related to the old Spanish adventurer who sailed so far up the '*River of Silver?*'"

"I should judge, my dear," interposed old Sister Hardiman, "that he was related to nothing Spanish, unless it was the Spanish Inquisition."

"Why," said Sister Wallet, "I always used to think Brother Cabot a very good man, and a good local preacher. He had a very lamb-like countenance."

"Very true, my dear," replied the old lady, "he did, at times, look like a lamb; but he could hate like a dragon."

"Well," said Sister Wallet, "you used to know him before I did, 'way back, when he was the regular preacher on the circuit. He certainly did seem to be unfortunate, for he had a fuss with first one, then another."

"With *all*, my dear; with first one, and

then another, because they were not all here at once; but, in the end, with all. Having left the work of the regular ministry, he always afterward seemed to be vexed with himself, and to take it out of those who were still in the way of regular duty."

"Well, how?" said one of the young ladies; "how could he trouble them? they were not obliged to mind him."

"It is an easy thing, my dear, for a man of not much force to make trouble. The people are too willing to be furnished with an excuse for not doing their duty. One of the best and holiest men we ever had, would have been starved out, had it not been for Clay and the blacks. Brother Cabot withdrew his own contribution, his influence, and did all he could to make the preacher leave from sheer necessity. But the brother weathered it out to the end of the year."

"O!" exclaimed Sister Wallet, "that reminds me: did not Brother Cabot have a great fuss with somebody, and write a pamphlet about it?"

"He had a great fuss," replied the old lady, "with everybody, about every thing, during all the time he was among us, which was more than twenty years; and nearly broke himself writing pamphlets and getting pieces put into the newspaper. O, it was a great mercy—the greatest mercy the circuit ever had—that took him away!"

"Well, Grandma, did you all do better after he left?"

"Not much, my dear. We had peace, but not much more plenty. I remember a most lovely young man who was sent here as the preacher, who always reminded me of the young man in the gospel whom Christ, looking at, loved; only this one, when called, did *not* turn away sorrowful; for his friends did all they could, but in vain, to keep him from becoming an itinerant preacher. He was well educated, unpretending in his manners, tall and handsome in his person, and of most undoubted piety. He was of delicate constitution, and he died in six months, of yellow fever. And there at Postville he lies, in an old graveyard that is without a fence. The circuit preacher told me the other day that he went to see his grave; that he found a place which looked like a common, except here and there an old crumbling brick tomb and some cypress stabs. On one of these stabs he found the initials 'W. H.' —O!" said the old lady, weeping, "Brother Hymes seemed to me as a son." Presently she continued, "But, worse than that, the circuit never paid the expenses of his funeral, which, being yellow fever time, were considerable; though the circuit owed him twice that amount when he died. I did what I could, but could only raise a small part of the sum. His parents sent down and paid the bill."

"I declare! what a shame!" said one of the young ladies.

"Ah! my child, if it were possible, my heart has grown used to such bitter, burning shame. I sometimes fear it has. I am afraid our people have grown used to money-meanness. O, how different from Mr. Wesley: from that old Methodism, and that yet older Christianity, which gave all, which laid all at the apostles' feet, and shared all things in common with the Lord's poor!"

"Why, Grandma, you do not mean to say," said another young lady, "that such cases are common in our Church?"

"Too common, my dear. We once had sent us a lovely young preacher and his wife, who had a sweet little flaxen-haired girl of two years. They were both very gifted and useful; the wife, if any thing, rather the more so of the two. She had been well educated, and knew well how to adapt herself to the variety of people with whom she met; and it was well she did, for they boarded round. O!" said the old lady, "I hate the very word—*boarded round.* In the summer she was taken down with fever; and, as it happened, at the time they were living in the house of a family who were absent travelling. While she was still sick the family returned. It was thought she could safely be moved to other quarters, and it was done; but she died in three days. I never shall forget her death. She had her child placed in front of her on the bed. When her sight was getting dim she gazed on her little darling intently, while smile after smile passed over her face. 'My dear husband,' said she, 'don't weep so: the Lord is so good to me. I leave you my likeness in our darling pet. My precious Saviour! how shall I ever praise thee enough? Kiss me, my dear! O, don't weep! I am so happy! How strange that this should be the sweetest moment of my life! What a soft light! Is it not the rainbow of his throne?' Such sublime rapture lighted her countenance and filled the very room where she died, that it did not seem as if it was death we witnessed, but the departure of an angel who had been here on a visit."

"But it was too bad to have moved her while she was so ill," said one of the ladies.

"Ah! my child, bad enough, if it did but affect us the right way. These things may make us exclaim or weep: do they make us give? Shall we still hear of 'widows' mites,' and try to make the people believe that they are to have the gospel without charge? I solemnly challenge any one to show any thing in the Jewish Dispensation which offers to teach life at a less cost than one fourth of the income of our farms or merchandise; or any thing in the teaching of Christ which contemplates any thing less than a fourth. The difference between the two dispensations is against these economists: Christ's teaching and example enforce not the gift of a fourth, but of all. The doctrine of the 'widow's mite' is the doctrine of *all you have.* It is sheer deception, positive misstatement in the mouths of most who use the word. Thank God, there are amongst Methodists a few noble exceptions, and that too amongst rich planters and rich merchants, as well as amongst poor ones; but their name is not legion. I never shall forget a scene that occurred some years since, in our church at Oakville. I believe several of you were there. Well, never mind, it will show both the bad and the good of this matter to these young sisters."

"O, do let us hear it, Grandma!" said they.

"Our circuit preacher that year was a very modest man, that knew nothing of the world, and would have starved outright be fore he would have told his wants to any one unasked. His wife was for all the world just like himself. They had but one child, an intelligent, delicate boy of about five years. In the summer, when most of the society was away, the little fellow began to droop, and presently to sink. The doctor said that the most that was needed was a change of air, and told his father—in the presence of Brother Jerry Larkum, as it happened—to take him at once to the sea-shore. Brother Jerry spoke up and said that could easily be done, as the boat which left once a week for the sea-shore would be at the landing the next day, and asked the preacher if he needed any funds. Brother Fielder smiled, and told him that his inquiry was opportune, as he had that day spent nearly the last cent for medicine. It seems that he waited on Brother Jerry: meanwhile Jerry mounted his horse, rode out home, and paid no more attention to the matter. Next day the boat left, but without the preacher. In a week the little boy died. It happened that Brother Goodsine was off at the time. I had not heard a word of the whole of it, living then, as I did, out on the road to Postville; and only by accident heard that the funeral was to be. I came in town just in time to attend it. There was no exhorter or local preacher present. Sister Fielder wept as though her heart would break; but Brother Fielder was singularly calm. He took the book, he said, more to draw comfort from God for himself and his dear wife than to perform the funeral-service for his own child. He read one verse: '*Are not two sparrows sold for a farthing? and one of them shall not fall on the ground without your Father.*' As he was about to begin, a little girl, Caroline Badger, went up to the table and placed some beautiful rosebuds on the breast of the little corpse. This unnerved him: he stooped down and kissed the little girl very affectionately. He presently mastered his feelings, and began: 'Our little Walter,' said he, 'used to fill this house all day with his play and voice, and it seemed to us the sweetest music in the world. But now, here he lies, all hushed in death! O, my friends! my little boy had a wonderful hold on his mother's heart and mine. And his death, I am persuaded, was not without the notice of our Heavenly Father; and I ought to be satisfied; and should be, could I only feel that it was not in part my own fault. He should have been taken to the sea-shore; and I confess it to you that it may ease my heart, I was too proud to ask help. Yes, too proud to save the life of my darling boy! The Lord forgive me!' Just then John Bear sprang forward, put his arms about his neck, and wept aloud. 'O, my dear minister! why were you so unkind as not to tell me about it?' As he stood there, his fine, rough face wet with tears, his large frame trembling with emotion, his hand upon Brother Fielder's shoulder, I could but think, even amid the anguish of the scene, that Brother Bear was the most noble-looking man I ever saw."

"And so he *is* one of the most noble-looking men *I* ever saw," said one of the young ladies; "and I shall not only admire Mr. Bear after this for his looks, but love him for his great heart. But, Grandma, are you done? I hope not."

"Yes, my dear, I ought to be; I have talked for two solid hours; but I could not sew, and you started a theme that affects me more than any other—this terrible blot upon the escutcheon of our Church: her systematic, cold neglect of the wants of her preachers, of her worn-out ministers, like old Father Hemphill, and of the widows and orphans of those that have died in the work: though I have only touched one branch of this subject."

"But, Grandma," replied the young lady,

"you must allow that some good has come out of sewing-societies—at least *our* sewing-society. It has given us a chance to hear the history of the poor money-policy of our circuit; and I am sure it will make *me* give ten times, yes, a hundred times, as much as I ever felt it my duty to give before."

"I sincerely hope it may, my dear," said the old lady.

CHAPTER V.

THE FIRST AND LAST AGONY.

THE first and the fourth Quarterly Conferences are among the times that try Methodist-men's souls. They are occasions on which human nature becomes manifest and all nature becomes human. At the first, the amount is estimated which is to be raised for the year for the support of the preachers and the presiding elder; and the fourth is the sounding of the last horn; the very last hour for doing justice; the time when the whole sum of dreadful deficiency stands out, confessed; and the precise instant when the last glimmer of hope for the unpaid balance expires. The first usually calls for long heads; the fourth, for long faces. Strong men, that are strong in faith out of doors, become weak as children in the same faith in a first Quarterly Conference. Men, who are often taken for pillars of the Church when sitting in the church responsive to the minister and happy in religion, become weaker than a bruised reed when the year's expenses are under consideration in a first Quarterly Conference. No man gets happy then, whatever he may do thereafter. The first Quarterly Conference is truly a trying time:

"Is n't it a trying time!
Is n't it a trying time!
A trying time, I say:
Is n't it a trying time!"
(*Negro Hymn.*)

But the fourth Quarterly Conference is a solemn time.

"Is n't it a solemn time!
Is n't it a solemn time!
A solemn time, I say:
Is n't it a solemn time!"
(*Negro Hymn.*)

Yet the sufferings of a Quarterly Conference are so ordered, that all its members do not suffer at the same time. One part of them suffer at the first Conference; the other, at the last. Those who feel that they owe a duty to themselves and their families as well as to the Church, suffer in the hour of making the estimates—at the first quarter: those who feel that they owe a duty to the Church as well as to themselves and their families, usually suffer in the hour of settlement—at the last quarter. The first Conference demands more nerve: the last, more grace. Many official members, therefore, who attend well second and third Quarterly Conferences, should scarcely be expected at either of these two. It is not every official member that is constituted so as to stand every thing.

The presiding elder of the district that included the Post-Oak Circuit had come up to his present official position, if not through much tribulation, yet certainly through many first and fourth Quarterly Conferences. He followed the Discipline in taking charge, not only of all the elders and deacons, travelling and local preachers and exhorters, but in supervising the temporal interests of the Church. He held the Quarterly Conference up to its duty in the premises, and the stewards to their responsibility to the Conference. "All men in this country, my brethren," he once addressed them, "both in Church and in State, are made responsible to some one for their official acts; and they should be held to that responsibility. It is the genius of all good government. No man is fit to hold office who does not recognize this principle clearly, or who is not willing to abide by it."

This was the second year he had presided over the circuit. At his first coming, he suggested to the stewards that possibly they might pursue a better policy than the one they proposed; but they were strong in the faith of a hundred failures—at least, Brother Badger was. Rubbing his hands in a gleeful way, and talking of "Doctor Bunting" and Mr. Wesley, shillings and pennies, sunbeams and mites—"Hand, do ye see! all seas are but rivers, and all rivers are but brooks, and all brooks are but rain-drops—small rain-drops!" Without inquiring particularly, it was easy for the elder to suppose, which he did, that some new element of success had probably been evolved by the labor and example of such a hearty representative of the universal drainage system which had been kept up so effectively by the English Wesleyans.

At the winding up of the year, however—the great financial *denouement*—his eyes were opened; and he saw that the circuit had, like the disciples, toiled all night and caught nothing. He determined to try and have things another way this year. Brother Blackman was not of that order of presiding elders who reckon a quarterly meeting and a Quarterly Conference a mere matter to be got through with quarterly. He magnified these occasions, both by his power in the pulpit, and the patient, minute, and serious attention which he gave to the temporal and disciplinary affairs of the circuit. His visits were a treat to the societies; and the people, both in the church and out of it, came to look with pleasing expectation for a quarterly meeting. A judge of the United States does not make the circuit of his courts with greater consciousness of the importance of the interests committed to his care than did Brother Blackman make the round of his district.

Thus, by the time of this, the first quarterly meeting of his second year, official members, with or without nerve, had come to understand that their presence on such official occasions was officially expected and required.

The meeting-house where the Quarterly Conference was about to be held was a frame of thirty by fifty, which stood a few hundred yards out of the town of Oakville proper. The "town," as it was called, consisted of not as many houses as there were letters in its name. Several of the houses were neatly enclosed and freshly painted, giving it an air of comfort and enterprise. The church, however, was worn, and seemed to have steadily declined all propositions for repairs or paint, and, with Methodistic plainness, to have resisted even the ordinary vanity of whitewash. The front-steps were rotted almost down. The old house wore a heartless look inside. It seemed to be no sanctuary for human weakness. Its slat-seats, its altar, and pulpit, were the natural color of the wood, modified only by time and preaching. It might have been imagination (or was it the law of association?) which suggested those scenes to which the old church had been a silent witness, if not a party: the desperate steward's-meetings, with their minutiæ of provision, their cold calculations, and their cruel deficiencies: "That is the best we can do, brother: we can't raise another cent: the people have been begged to death to get this much." O what agonies of fourth quarterly meetings! the poor preacher, mild with desperation, taking the little scrapings of silver with so few words of complaint, that, to the stewards, his case did not seem so very hard after all: these things might have made against the old place, with its dark scantling, and joists, and weather-boarding, all looking as if they had drunk in the light of many a tear, and were thirsty still. Such thoughts quite overpowered the better class of associations which, to a certain extent, the old house might have claimed to suggest; for its history was not entirely devoïd of good meetings and sacred influences.

Several horses were hitched to the willow-oaks and chinas which shaded the church. A middle-size person, wearing a preacher's hat, rode up. The animal he rode was a bay mare. She had a full eye, straight neck, small head, ample breast, clean limbs, mole-skin hair, and barrel-shaped body; which, since the days of Virgil, have been the sure marks of a good horse. Her neck was bleeding in a dozen places, as if it had been lanced. The horseman, as he rode up, was greeted by a portly, tall personage, who wore a broad-rimmed white hat.

"How do you, Brother Larkum? Why, bless me! how the flies have cut your mare!"

"Why, yes, Squire, that's a fact, they have; they have indeed—not deep, and not much comes, but it hurts, like a church-collection."

"Ah, Brother Larkum, we have both felt that sting," rejoined the tall personage, putting in the last word with some vacancy.

"That seems to be an animal of fine spirits."

"Spirits! why, Squire, she sees them; and no ways fractious neither. I sometimes think, Squire, that our horses are more solemn than we."

"Have you heard the news of the death of my Selim?" asked the Squire.

"Misery Moses! no! you don't tell me! That *was* a fine horse! It always reminded me of 'Whitey and the General' to see you on him."

"He was more of a pale horse than a white," said the Squire; "in fact, that horse, as you say, *was* solemn: he cost me three hundred dollars. Death has been among us, you know."

To this speech, which was spoken with emphasis, and a gaze as if the speaker watched its effect, the horseman shook his head with an altered countenance, and said nothing. He adjourned the conversation by dismounting and tying his mare to the branch of an oak sapling.

Besides those officials who have been named, there had gathered some four or five from the Postville end of the circuit, several from "The Flats" meeting-house, from "Crane's School-house," from "Hunnicuts," and from "The Belluses"—societies making up the circuit, and which spread over a considerable extent of country. These were, in the main, like other class-leaders and stewards. The only exceptions were "the two Belluses," as they were generally called: one, a large, pursy man; the other, a small, dried man, as unlike his brother in looks as was possible to be. The two were, however, very much alike in good nature, and thought about the same quantity on every subject, which was not much. Each was a great admirer of the other, and was perfectly satisfied in all matters of opinion if he had his brother for an opponent; which he was sure to have, for there seemed to be a tacit understanding between them never at the same time to take the same side of any question. When Brother Sam, or "Big Bellus," as his neighbors called him, spoke, Brother Jake shook his head at the first opinion which his brother might "spend," and at the same time looked about surprised and winking, as much as to say, "It won't do: you see it won't do." So with Sam, when Jake spoke: only, he looked about, smiling and winking. But all this was in talk; in practice and habit they were as alike as two peas.

"Jim Hunnicut" was also something of a character. He often said that he did not pretend to be much of a Christian; that he loved Methodism because it was the People's Church. He was of middle stature, impulsive, a good talker, generous, and had been sent to the Legislature once, upon the merit of being one of the cleverest fellows in the county. He constituted that link between the Church and the world which most every "society" furnishes.

"Old Clay," the natural representative of the colored society of Oakville, was present, upon the great principle of taxation *with* representation; for the Badger-policy had looked to the negroes to help out the support of the circuit. Brother Oakhart did all the out-loud talking in regard to matters that concerned his charge.

As the elder neared the church, walking from the village, a bare-headed negro boy, riding a mule bare-back, or, rather, on an empty corn-sack, with a rope-bridle, approached, and, with a tug at his uncombed and uncombable wool, in place of taking off a hat, he presented a letter. While opening the letter, the elder asked the boy after his master's health, and looked at the mule and his rider. The boy's skin looked husky, and, clothes and all, as if slightly convalescent from a severe attack of sackcloth and ashes. The mule looked as if it had been fed for three months on long-moss. After glancing through the letter: "Your master says you've all had pretty hard times lately."

"Well, massa, we has, sir; indeed, sir, we has, indeed," said the boy.

"Well, are you going straight back?"

"Yes, sir: I'se going down to the store for some meal; then I'se going right back, sir."

"Tell your master I am sorry he has had such a hard time, and I hope to see him next time, at next quarterly meeting: now carry a straight message; do you hear? I'm sorry, and hope he'll come next time."

"I'll be certain to tell him, sir: good-morning, massa."

As the boy rode off, the elder took a second look at the epistle. It read:

"REV. T. BLACKMAN, Presiding Elder:

DEAR BROTHER: I can't come to your

quarterly meeting. My mules is very bad off with charbone. One is dead. This year my crops is all gone. The bole-worm has got my crop. I have a continual hurting across my misery, which also keeps me from coming to the meeting. I send you two fifty cents, one quarter, one dime, two five cents, all wrapped up inside of this. I can't come.

"Pray for
"Your needy
"And absent brother.
"ISAAC STOKES."

When the elder entered the church, Brother Wallet and several of the brethren from a distance were finishing, in slow metre, a rather ominous hymn:

"Hark! from the tombs, a doleful sound:
Mine ears, attend the cry."

The opening hymn, which the elder read

in a thoughtful, impressive manner, was that fine one, beginning:

"Jesus, my Lord, how rich thy grace!
Thy bounties, how complete!
How shall I count the matchless sum?
How pay the mighty debt?"

Brother Jerry Larkum, who seemed to have a foreboding of by-and-by, and determined to seize the present for his demonstration, was quite transported with the hymn, and gave way audibly to his handkerchief and his feelings while the last two lines were sung:

"O, rather let me beg my bread,
Than keep it back from thee."

The elder showed plainly by his prayer that he thought the shouting-time had not yet arrived. He prayed with great fervor to God for pardon for their sins—sins of omission; that during the past year they had received the pure word of the gospel, at the hands of a man devoted to its ministry; that they had received blessings—blessings upon themselves and their firesides—but had returned little, exceeding little, to God, the Church, or the minister. He dwelt upon the grace of Him who, though he was rich, yet for our sakes became poor, that we through his poverty might be rich; upon the self-denial of those by whom the gospel had come down to us. He called up the unfulfilled vows of those present to give all to his service, as witnesses against such as have sworn deceitfully to the God of their salvation; and so continued until the whole Conference felt the power of a good man's prayer. Brother Jerry evidently found no crevice in it in which he could chirp, and so was thoroughly searched and sobered.

Brother Badger was chosen the secretary, and proceeded on in the record of the regular questions and answers, until the elder asked, "What provision has been made on this circuit for the support of the preacher in charge and the presiding elder?"

"I must say, Brother Blackman," said one of the Postville leaders, "I think that the Bishop was rather hard on us this year: we are not very strong, noways."

"It is right hard on us, it is so," chimed in another; "but," he added, "I suppose He will temper the wind to the shorn lamb!"

"Last year," said Hunnicut, "I doubt if our fleece paid for the shearing."

"Why, my dear brethren," said the elder, "what is the matter? You have a preacher, and I hope a very good one."

"Ay, as to that," said Brother Badger, "we all think him a proper man. But the support, do ye see! six mouths, and every mouth eats bread."

"Last year," said the elder, "you had a man and his wife, and did not support them. I thought that if you had more to do, you would do more. The circuit is wealthy enough to support two preachers with families easily. And now, brethren, I wish you to have a free conversation while we are upon this matter of estimate and finance: what do you propose?"

"It is a great pity," said a leader from "the Flats," "that we could not have a single man: we should have struck out very rank this year; we should have come through very handy."

"I should suppose," said Jake Bellus, "that the elder might yet swap him off for a single man. What, Brother Sam, no? well, *I* think he might, if he would." But Sam's head was not to be stopped by explanation. "I mean to say, he should if he would; and should he not, if he could? if not, then he should not; certainly he should not."

"I can't think he should not swap him if he could," replied Sam Bellus; "and if he could not, how should he? I say *this*, even if he should; and if he could not, or should not, I am sure he would not; certainly he would not."

"I hope, Mr. President," said Hunnicut, "those brethren over there understand each other."

"I understand," said the elder, "they differ as to whether I might, could, would, or should swap the preacher off. But the question is, how much are you going to allow your preacher this year? Come to the point, brethren."

"The last crop," said a brother from "the Flats," "was very light, and the stand this year is the poorest *I* ever saw: I am afraid there will be poor picking our way for preacher or people."

"I know down *our* way," said a brother from Crane's, "we are expecting just nothing pretty much."

"That will be enough to pay your quarterage, brother," said Hunnicut, "if you intend to pay the same this year that you did last."

"How many children has the brother?" said a member; "because I thought maybe if he had not too many, maybe he might board round. We could board him about Postville a right smart while, and it would not come heavy on us neither—a week or so apiece."

"It would be very handy to *us*," said another, from "the Flats."

"It would come somewhat hard on us," said a "Crane" member; "but I suppose we could stand it for a day or two all round. We are willing to do what we can," said he, sighing, "for the support of the gospel; but we are rather light-handed down our way."

"Well, brethren," said the elder, "you need hardly discuss that, for I understand your preacher to say that he cannot consent to board so large a family round."

"Maybe some of his children are large enough to help themselves," said one from "Crane's."

"They are all small," responded the elder.

"We had a preacher here once," said one from the Postville end: "my! what a smart wife he had! She was the smartest, handiest woman about a house, and sewing, and such like, that was ever on the circuit. I think one of the stewards boarded her in part for what sewing she could do."*

"I don't think the stewards can hire out the preacher's wife this year," replied the elder; "though I know her to be a very smart wife—perhaps too smart for such an arrangement. I think, brethren, you had better come to figures. What amount do you wish to raise?"

"Where will he live, if he keeps house?" said one. "I know of a good vacant house, that needs some repair, in Postville, a little

* The writer has it from good authority that, once on a time, the stewards of —— Circuit, in the —— Conference, actually did this very thing.

ways out of town. It would not cost much to make it so he could live in it."

"How far is it from town?" asked the elder.

"Well, I should judge about half a mile."

"Yes," said another, "I think that house might be got for a trifle. The fences are gone, but it could easily be made comfortable. The people that used to live there disliked it on account of the funerals; but I suppose a preacher would not mind that."

"It occurs to me," interposed the elder, "that if you allow your preacher enough to live on, as I suppose you will, he can suit himself in that matter. Come, begin with items, Brother Badger."

The great base-line was accordingly run: that is, the Disciplinary allowance put down, as follows:

"Disciplinary allowance for preacher,	$150.00
" " for wife,.........	150.00
Three children under seven, $25 each,	75.00
One child over seven,......................	40.00
Travelling expenses to circuit,..........	50.00."

"Now, how much for table expenses?" asked the elder; "what does it cost you brethren in Oakville? what does it cost you, Brother Badger?"

"Well," answered Brother Badger, (who was a notorious good liver,) "if ye mean the victuals, and the wood, and the servants, and the rent, and keeping a horse, and a cow, and a carriage, why, do ye see! I am not able to say just now."

"No," said the elder, "I want only the item of marketing and groceries."

"Well, now, really ye are too hard for me," answered the secretary. "Mrs. Badger, do ye see! she manages most of these things."

"I suppose," said the elder, "you want your preacher to live as well as you do yourself, Brother Badger: I am very sure of *that*. Does it cost you five dollars a week for marketing, and twenty dollars a month for groceries?"

"Yes, I suppose," answered Brother Badger.

"Does it not cost you twice that?" said the elder.

"Well, Mrs. Badger, do ye see! she manages all this; but I dare say, possibly it does: I can't make sure."

"Then I think," said the elder, "we are safe in adding,

"Marketing, at $5 a week, ...$260.00
Groceries, at $20 a month, ... 240.00.

What for wood? shall I say two dollars a month? that's low; well, put that down.

"Fuel, ...$25.00.

What for servants? What do you pay for field-hands, Brother Wallet? 'Twelve dollars a month:' well, put that down:

"One servant to cook and wash, say......$120.

If you want your preacher's wife to visit you, she ought to have a little girl to help nurse the baby: what do you say for that?"

"O," said a brother, "she can get a small girl most anywhere for nothing."

"Good for nothing, you might better say," said Hunnicut.

"Well," continued the elder, "put down also,

"Small girl for nurse,......................$30.00.

What now about the horse? your preacher has to keep a horse, and, when home, in his own stable. What do you sell corn for, Brother Badger? 'A dollar:' well, suppose we say,

"Horse-feed,..............................$25.00?

The cow we'll hope some of you will lend. Now for the house-rent."

"How much does all that add up, Mr. President?" said a brother.

Brother Badger answered, "Eleven hundred and sixty-five dollars."

"I think, Mr. President," said a steward from "Crane's," "we are getting pretty well up in the figures."

"Well, brother," replied the elder "it is high time you were getting up in them; you have been down long enough."

"I don't know," said a steward from "the Flats," "but I thought we strained our prettiest last year: didn't we, Brother Badger? and it all counted up only four hundred and fifty dollars. I somehow fear that we are putting all that down there on paper. I am afraid we can't do it: I wish we could."

"For my part," said one from the Postville end, "I am willing to do my best, and that is not much; but it's mighty hard to raise money these times. By the time the fifth collection is lifted, and the missionary apportionment, and the Bible collection, and the Christian Advocate, is paid for, and all this on the top of the circuit preacher's allowance, the people have pretty much lost all spirit, and complain mightily; and it naturally sets them against the sight of we stewards."

"Well, brother," said the elder, opening a blank-book, "I have a note here of the drain your society at Postville suffered last year: it raised,

"For the preacher,	$50.00
For the Bible cause,	10.00
For the Fifth Collection,	3.75
For missions,	18.75
	$82.50

Say eighty-two dollars and fifty cents. You take there five copies of the Advocate, which, at two dollars a year, can hardly be reckoned a charity: all told, not one hundred dollars, which is not as much as I hope we shall receive this year from you alone; for I believe you make from fifty to seventy-five bales of cotton: one tenth of that, which ought to be sacred to the Lord, would be, say six bales, or three hundred dollars; and surely you will not do less than one third of what you ought to do. I understand that the society at Postville make at least, all together, not less than five hundred bales; and if it gives only one hundred dollars or less a year, I don't wonder the people have not much spirit left."

"I am sure of one thing," said Brother Sam Bellus; "that the sound of them high figures will go very far at first to throw the people into a despair, or (looking at Jake) into a sort of a state to make up their minds what they will do or not, as I may say, at a word; and I think differently from what Brother Jake thinks: I think they will be most sure to do it, I really do. In that case I don't think that they will object to do all they can, which, I fear, will not be much, at least not as much as my brother here thinks it will be; though I cannot agree with him—I certainly cannot—that the people will not do their very prettiest: that is, if they don't take a scare first, which I am pretty much certain they will be most sure to do."

"I hope," exclaimed Hunnicut, "that no one will speak until Brother Jake Bellus has an opportunity to explain!"

The fact was, that when one of them spoke, the other was so certain to follow, that no person ever pretended to come in between. John Bear used to say, that the two Belluses were confusion confounded: that Sam always confused, and Jake always confounded.

Brother Jake responded, that he could not be sure of the fact that his brother had just alluded to—he wished he could—in reference to the people taking a scare at the high figures. He was afraid they would not take a scare at first, but that they would afterwards take a scare; which, in his opinion, would be worse than if they took an early scare: that possibly they might (looking at Sam) do as his brother thought: in that case they would be most sure to do all that they could, though he did not think they would; but he did think, that if they should do what they could at first, that the scare that they might take would not make so much difference: that is, if they did what he thought they would do, which was, that they would do their prettiest before they took a scare; which he was very certain they would be most sure not to do.

Hunnicut arose, and said gravely, that he could not agree with either of the brothers Bellus, though he could most fully with both of them. He thought that the people would either take a scare before they did their prettiest, or they would do their prettiest before they took a scare; and in either case they would do their prettiest, and if they did *that*, he supposed that no one would object to their taking a scare just when they pleased, whether before or after.

"After that, I think," said the elder, "we can proceed to estimate the house-rent. How much ought it to be—two hundred dollars?

Well, if you all think that about right, put it down, Mr. Secretary:

"House-rent,........................$200.00.

"That is, expenses for the year—without allowing for contingencies of any kind, or for laying up one cent, which every man in this country hopes to do, but which Methodist preachers, and nearly all ministers of the gospel of every denomination, leave for ever out of the question—are thirteen hundred and sixty-five dollars.

"How much, Brother Wallet, do you give your overseer, besides finding him a house and food for his family? 'One thousand dollars.' Well, no doubt he earns it. How much, Brother Badger, do you give your bookkeeper? 'Fifteen hundred dollars.' Well, no doubt you can well afford to do it. And should not a man who devotes himself to the ministry have support at the rate of the superintendent of a plantation or a principal clerk? What say you, brethren?

Tell me, you who have grown rich yourselves by paying your employés these prices, is not the man you are willing to sit under as your minister and the minister of truth and morals to your children, entitled to as much from you as they? This is what your preacher ought to have, and if you have the hearts of men, if the hearts of men of God, you will give him every cent of it. It is an obligation you owe to God, but not the less to the minister who devotes himself to your interests as a church. The question, *How* will you raise it? is secondary. The first thing for you to do is—as men of honesty, as the leaders of the people, as they who have received 'another spirit,' who have at one time vowed to God your all—resolve that this *shall be* done. It is a debt you incurred when you became members of the Church—the body of Christ—to support the gospel; and one that you cannot place second to any claim."

As the Conference adjourned to meet after preaching, and all the brethren were very much exhausted, the "First Agony" may properly be divided into two chapters.

CHAPTER VI.

HOLD YOUR PURSE AND KEEP YOUR COUNTENANCE.

THE first man to speak after the Conference came to order was Brother Jerry Larkum. He said that the talk of the elder this morning had been to him a very solemn drum-call to duty. He hoped that the church would no longer drag her glory, but now unfold her gold-feathers, and proudly shiver them before the eyes of a smit-public. The brethren would no doubt bear in mind that he had been now trying for better than a twelvemonth in his weak way to stir and skim; and if he could not get things to a boil, he thought he had more than once brought them to a simmer. What he might have done, be it little or be it much, he was willing to throw it all in: he should never bring any charge himself, but when he had seen the plate of solicitation going the round, and then coming back a plate of clean-disappointment, it had given him the heart-chronics; "which was, you know," said he, "brethren, a very crank feeling to go sprangling over a man just after exercising."

"I hope, Mr. President," said Hunnicut, "that inasmuch as Brother Jerry is going to *give* the church all the benefit of his labors, his contribution will be as large this year as it has always been."

"How will you make up this amount, brethren, which you are to raise for your preacher?" asked the elder. "My claim on you for this year is one hundred dollars, which will make in all that you are to raise fourteen hundred and sixty-five dollars.

How will you get it? What say you, Brother Badger?"

Brother Badger had held his peace astonishingly during the meeting. He seemed to be in an amazement of financial exaggeration—things had gone beyond his habitual depth. Indeed, a gulf of estimates yawned, which he saw at a glance was large enough to swallow his "sunbeams," "mites," and "pennies," and be a gulf still. "Do ye see! the sum is very large, I may say a very large sum for the Post-Oak: I suppose we must try—we can but try, and when we have done what we have, why, do ye see! we can do no more!"

"Put it down, brother, put it down in figures," said the elder. Brother Badger put down and down—" Crane's, $25 ; Hunnicut's, $50 ; Postville, $100 ; Oakville, $250 ; Belluses', $25 ; The Flats, $25. Total, $475."

"How will you raise the remainder, brother?"

"Well, I have put down the most they can carry, and, do ye see! it's the last feather does the damage."

"Brother Badger has a great reputation our way, sir, as a financier," said Hunnicut; "he is not easily scared—mountains are with him but molehills."

"I hope, then, he will not make these molehills mountains," said the elder.

"No, no," said the secretary, "I am not for discouraging ye—that will come soon enough of itself—but I am thinking that our mountain here will be like the hancient one that brought forth a mole."

"A mouse!" interposed Hunnicut.

"Well, well," replied Brother B., "they are much of a size; and it's the size we are taking account of now. I suppose there is something from Brother Oakhart's people—another $25; and there is the sewing-society—but I expect no such hextraordinary providence in that way as we had last year;

(Brother Wallet shook his head ;) and so that will not be more than $15; then there is a strawberry party—we had it once, and it yielded a good bit, some $25; and there 's an old-country tea-drinking at the preacher's house, with something neat wrapped up left under the plate—that was allowed at $20; and there is a chance we had last year, and might have it again—I can 't say—a sacred painting of a Noah's Ark, and the children of Israel with their harps on the willows in the city of Babylon, and a Daniel in the Lion's Den: all very pious and proper, if it would come along, and so it might—I can 't say—and it yielded some $20; and, indeed, in many ways has Providence opened the way for us, and may again—I can 't say. Well, there is a fair could be held, which might bring us in a trifle of maybe $30; or it, along with a *Tab-Low Vevong*, say $35; and that, I suppose, is about all."

"Could we not, somehow, have a raffle,

Brother Badger?" interposed a brother from Crane's; "that's a mighty good way, I think, for making things come light all round."

"Sure enough," replied the secretary, who was caught napping, "I had forgotten that;" but added very promptly, "Though ye'd hardly reckon the preacher and his family a prize! and, do ye see, there'd be nothing else to raffle."*

---

* The brother from Crane's and the secretary scarcely dreamed of the extent to which lotteries have been sanctified to the use of the Church. The following, from one of the Advocates, shows to what a pitch the indirect method of raising supplies can be brought, under the benign auspices of Saint Luck:

"*Consecrated Lotteries.*—The Roman Catholic Church in France still resorts to gambling for its maintenance, as may be seen by the following extract from a late letter to the Christian Advocate, by the Rev. Abel Stevens:

"The newspapers have been constantly crowded with advertisements of consecrated lottery programmes, and no little interest prevails here from the fact that tomorrow (16th of August) the lottery of St. Rock has its drawing. It has a capital of 1,200,000 francs, 25,000 of which will be distributed in prizes among

"Then you will have," said the elder, "from all these sources, supposing that Providence smiles upon you on all sides, $140; which, added to $475, would be a total of $615, which is *not* ($1365) the amount we want. What next?"

---

49 drawing numbers. One ticket, costing only 20 cents, can draw 140,000 francs, or, in other words, $28,000. This splendid gambling project has been formed for the purpose of erecting a new church at Montpelier to St. Rock, who was born there. It has the sanction of the government, and will have its drawing under the auspices and with the responsibility of a state officer. But above all, it has received a special grace from his Holiness the Pope, which is duly announced in the advertisements as a bait to the faithful. Now, this is but an example of what is occurring incessantly, though on a less commanding scale, throughout France. Individual parishes get up these lotteries for local purposes: most generally, the prizes are not money, but articles of taste, of dress, literature, or art. St. Sulpice, of this city, has recently had one in the gardens of the Luxembourg. Some of the most valuable articles were contributed by the cabinet minister of 'public worship and instruction,' who, indeed, seems very much given to this sort of patronage. They were on exhibition for weeks, as a temptation to the purchase of tickets."

For once, even the Brothers Bellus agreed, as they both shook their heads the same way; for all things in that Quarterly Conference, as one of the brethren expressed it, had come to a right dead stall. All were profoundly contemplative, except Hunnicut and one or two near him, who rather enjoyed the general nonplus. Immense plans rolled and rolled through the mind of the Quarterly Conference—then "melted into air, into thin air."

In good taste with so solemn a pause, Squire Wallet slowly arose. He said that he felt that the time had come for proposing what he had intended to propose these two years past. It was evident that the church needed help—help which no earthly power could give; "for," said he, "we are all weak." He would propose a new source of income, one that would be regulated by Providence, and one that naturally belonged to the Church—a graveyard: that the church should purchase a tract of poor land, cheap, and lay it off in burial-lots: that a great many people were dying, as he had occasion to know by his own sad experience, who would all want to be buried somewhere: that many of them were not choice; indeed, would prefer to be buried in a religious graveyard: that it would be certain to pay—many things were uncertain, but the grave was not: that the whole community would, in that case, become certain contributors to the gospel. The church might hope, sooner or later, to bury the entire town. And it would be a satisfaction to know that the very last money spent for a man in this life went into the church-treasury. He thought it was a duty which every man owed to society to save all he could out of the devouring grave. "O," exclaimed he,

'How populous, how vital is the grave!
This is creation's melancholy vault!'"

Hunnicut arose, and remarked, that the

squire had presented a very grave proposition, not unlike what he had expected from one who had so much experience in such matters: who had, since the loss of his thirty hands by cholera in '48, read every thing, as he believed, in the English classics, upon the subject of death and the grave, that was worth reading. (The squire nodded affirmatively.) Besides the pleasure which he felt in hearing such a proposition from so intelligent a source, he was glad that it had such an origin on another account. The squire, he said, had a very large number of hands, and, though he could not, of course, wish such a thing, yet, if the cholera should again come, could the church calculate on the squire's patronage? He would be glad to have an expression of opinion upon that point from one whom they possibly might look to as their largest customer.

The squire replied that it was not certain that he should need any grave-room this year. Besides, it was known to most of the brethren that he had his own little grave-patch behind his quarters, which he should be obliged to fill before he went elsewhere. "But," said he, in a generous, open way, "I will say this much to brethren: if I had half my niggers back, I would be willing to bury the rest in the graveyard of the church, and thanky', too."

Hunnicut said that he thought that was all that they could reasonably have asked, and that it was a very handsome offer, under the circumstances.

The Brothers Bellus were wide awake. The larger one, Brother Sam, said that that offer of the squire's struck him as very handsome—more so than any that he had ever heard of; that it had rolled a big burden off of his mind which the circuit expenses had rolled in on him. If the squire would furnish the circuit with niggers enough to do all the burying, and Providence would send a smart chance of sickness—and he thought he could not see why they should not have it—that then it, that is, the circuit, could, and he thought should, and no doubt would, soon bury itself clean out of debt.

Brother Jake said he could not agree with his brother. The squire's fine offer was a very fine offer for true; but it had not rolled any burden, or any part of any burden, off of him: it had rolled him under a burden, because it somehow struck him that if the squire should lend the circuit half his niggers to bury people with the cholera, that they would be most certain to take it; and the squire's hands would always die when they did; and then, that the circuit would have to pay some one to bury the squire's niggers, and would only just bury up the circuit in debt.

Hunnicut replied that he thought he could relieve the minds of the Brothers Bellus; that in no event could the squire's offer or the squire's negroes be any additional charge to the circuit, for those he had so generously offered to the church upon a certain contingency were already dead and buried. "I believe I am right, squire, am I not?"

The squire assented fully.

"Well, brethren," said the elder, "the support of your preacher is to depend upon subscriptions, collections, a sewing-society, a strawberry party, a tea-drinking, a fair, an itinerant exhibition of oil-paintings, a graveyard, and the cholera!"

"You forget us darkies," said Brother Oakhart: "Brother Badger counts a good deal on us."

"O yes, so I did: I should not have forgotten that, or the seamstress." He continued, "My dear brethren, it is impressed upon my mind, if we wish Providence to help us, we must at least try to help ourselves; and if you will permit me, I will suggest to you *A Method for raising the Cur-*

rent Expenses of the Circuit, which shall be both certain and regular in its operation; that is, if you will give it a fair trial."

Brother Jerry Larkum spoke up—that he was certain it was the very thing wanted, and that old Post-Oak would be as true to herself as ever. Jerry liked to back the elder.

"The stewards will please take this list of the members," said the elder, "which I have provided on purpose. They will please begin at themselves—the name of the oldest steward first—and then call the name of each member of the church, and say what, in their judgment, each one ought to give, in view of his ability, and the amount which the circuit is to raise this year."

"You are going to leave nothing for the goats," said a brother from Crane's; "they are stronger than we sheep down our way."

"Yes, I am," replied the elder: "the goats, as you call them, will come in good play for church cleaning, and to constitute a contingent fund, in case the sheep do not pay up. Call the names of the stewards, Brother Badger. 'Brother Goodsine:' how much ought Brother Goodsine to pay? I do not ask what he has paid, but what proportion of this thirteen hundred and sixty-five dollars ought he to pay, taking into view his yearly income and ability?"

One of the brethren thought that Brother Goodsine ought not, in truth and justice, to pay more than ten dollars; that he was no better off than himself, and *he* knew that was pretty near his own gauge.

Brother Goodsine remarked that if the brethren would put it down at fifty dollars, they could count on getting it.

"Well," said the elder, "I expect that is about right for Brother G. 'Brother Badger:' how much for him?"

They all agreed that Brother B. was worth ten times as much as Brother G.

Brother Badger remarked that this was all a new thing under the sun to him, and he had been a church steward some time.

"What have you credited yourself for last year, Brother B.? 'Fifteen dollars and seventy-five cents.' Well, brethren, shall Brother Badger be put down at that this year?"

Hunnicut said that Brother Badger and himself were good for a hundred each. So, after a good deal of hitching, it went down: "Bunting Badger, $100." After this style all of the stewards apportioned each other.

"Now," said the elder, "the stewards can apportion the amount expected from each member."

About the time Brother Jerry's name was to be called, he went to the window; then to the door: his mare was uneasy; he had to go out. After staying some time, he came in and said he was very much afraid she was taking a colic. Hunnicut whispered to him, "If she shows any signs of that, give her a ten-dollar gold-piece." Jerry was too good a judge of veterinary treatment not to take the hint.

How much for Brother Jeremiah Larkum? was asked. Jerry said that he wished the elder and the brethren to understand that he expected nothing for his exhorting; that he was always willing to do what he could, under grace.

"So we understand," said Hunnicut; "and I think that in view of that, and the value of Brother Jerry's fine bottom-land, he should be put down at least half as much as myself, though he is worth more than any of us, excepting the squire and Brother Badger."

The three brethren all looked grieved that, under such circumstances, they should be so regarded. But Jerry was put down at fifty dollars.

"Sister Lasey—what of her? she is very poor," asked one of the stewards.

"The method is," said the elder, "*to put*

something down for every one to do, if it only be two dollars and fifty cents a year. It will be very easy for some of you to give a widow that much privately. Teach all that it is a duty, that it is expected of them, to help support the gospel. In this country, a man must be poor indeed who cannot give ten dollars annually, or a woman that cannot give five dollars, for that purpose."

"But here," said one of the stewards, "is the name of Sister Williams. I hope nothing will be put down to her. She is the daughter of old Brother Hemphill, and has to support the old man, excepting what he gets from the Conference, which, last year was only twenty dollars."

"There, brethren," said the elder, "there is a man who for forty-five years was an active, useful itinerant preacher: now, in his old age, nearly blind, and helpless, the Methodist Church has cast him on his widowed daughter for a support! Our Church is not guilty of blood—only of ingratitude. Where are the men who were converted by the preaching of that man of power? Why, in the Church, to be sure; and many of them wealthy, and happy in religion! I* will see that Sister Williams pays you five dollars."

"I am altogether with the elder," said Brother Jerry. "The like of such should make us all weep. Many is the gill of salt tears that have rolled from my eyes like hot shot for the Conference orphans and widows. I have moaned over them until I have had in my own self, on account of that one thing, more hard suffering than a watering-place! But I don't complain for myself. If my toiling as an humble plenipotentiary is worth any thing, or is not worth any thing to my church, it shall all go."

* "Let our conduct for ever abolish the idea, now so extensively entertained in the churches, that we are, *ex officio*, excused from giving."—THE GREAT QUESTION.

"We all understand, Mr. President, that Brother Jerry's is a settled case," said Hunnicut: "the Church accepts his services at nothing, and only charges him this year fifty dollars."

"Brethren," continued the elder, "this is no light matter. The brother tells us he has shed tears; and no wonder. Tears, tears! Yes, the Church has shed tears, and has still tears to shed, over those who have done her good service, but who are now no longer able to serve her; and she has tears too for those who have given to her a father or a husband! But what are her tears—tears of gratitude or tears of economy? O, Church of my heart! thou that readest the prophets! thou that receivest them that are sent unto thee! O that thou, even thou, in all thy prosperity, hadst ministered to the declining hours of thy broken servants! but now they are gone! How couldst thou have visited their widows in affliction, and gathered their orphans together, as a hen gathereth her chickens under her wings, and wouldst not!"

The whole list was called, and each member in the circuit apportioned some part of the year's estimate.

"If any of you object to these sums, which your brethren think you ought to pay, do so when the stewards present this apportionment list to the membership and congregation; as some doubtless are set down at too little, and some at too much. On to-morrow,' continued the elder, "I shall request the entire membership to remain after church is dismissed, together with such persons as are willing to contribute to support the ministers on the circuit. Then we will read out, (1.) The whole amount to be raised this year for Post-Oak. (2.) The highest amount apportioned to any one. (3.) The lowest amount apportioned. (4.) The whole list. And be certain, if a man object to saying what he will do, or make an ado about being apportioned, or find fault with what he terms 'the principle of the thing,' as if it invaded the voluntary principle, you may set it down, as I do from long observation, that he does not wish certainly to pay any thing. Ninety-nine chances to one, his objections are only to cover the retreat of a covetous mind. What good reason can there be for not *saying* what share we will take of the cost of the gospel—unless it be singly the fear of the effect of our example? I have here, therefore, what I call quarterage notes: a rivet, something to hold. I have had a number printed on purpose. Hand them round."

"The elder," whispered Hunnicut, "carries his calomel along with him."

"Yes," returned John Bear, "and his jalap too."

The elder's "calomel and jalap" were printed:

"OAKVILLE, Feb. 1, 185 .

$________

"I promise to pay the STEWARDS of the Post-Oak Circuit, at some time during this year, the sum of ____________dollars, for the support of the METHODIST MINISTERS on this circuit.

"(Signed) ____________________.

"After all the members have heard how much they have been apportioned, then distribute these blank quarterage notes: explain that these notes are not bankable, but are to give the promise a tangible shape. Then *take time:* never attempt a collection in a hurry. Do not allow any singing: it is no time to sing. You need no Ashantee-drum to drown the groans of the wounded, where there are no human victims. Gather up your quarterage notes, read out the names and amounts subscribed. If the sum subscribed is not as large as you need, say so, and get some one to give a larger note. *Keep at it until you get the sum needed.* Then sing: 'sing praises to God, sing praises'—'sing ye praises with understand ing.'

"This, my brethren, is a 'plan,' a financial plan. And what are '*plans?*' Does generosity need a plan?—charity from the skies move only after a plan? No such thing. He that has much to sow sows broadcast. There is a man whose economy extends even to God; who would fain make the most of a little charity. Such a one is always ready to be one of a hundred to make up five hundred dollars. His effort to drag others along with him in his misery becomes a miserable drag. Such sow only in the drill, and then furnish only one seed in the row. Given a man with a Christian conscience, and you have a man with a 'plan' of charity in him that always works. Let there be offered by the Church a standing prize of five hundred dollars for every man that can be produced who has a correct sense of a

Christian's obligation to God to support and spread the gospel."

When the elder finished, Brother Oakhart said, "Mr. President, I and Brother Clay here haven't said any thing at this quarterly meeting, though we have had our own thoughts. Our mind is, that all that is wanted in this circuit, and most anywhere, is, when the people are money-difficulted, to get the nigger out of them. We know that there are white niggers as well as black ones. It is natural meanness, no matter what skin carries it. We are willing to do our part. The preacher sha'n't beg bread so long as we have any thing. No, sir: we will live on persimmons and craw-fish all the time sooner than not pay the preacher. You can count on us at the last stretch. We shall not fly the track."

"There is a good deal of truth in what Brother Oakhart has said," said Hunnicut.

"The brethren know that I make no pretension to being much of a Christian: I am sorry to say it; though I love the Methodist Church, because it preaches to the people. And, I suppose, I stand where I can take a worldly view of this whole matter of paying the preacher; not such a happy view as friend Jerry; nor such a grave view as the squire; nor such a widow's-mite view as Brother Badger; but a common view, as of any other business matter. Here we have been dodging and straining—to do what? Why, to raise a sum of money that any five of us would have put down for any other purpose in five minutes. Either of us would sign a note for a hundred dollars, or lend a hundred, or lose it, for most any man or any thing that comes along, and think nothing of it. I leave religion out of the question; and I say I want no man to give his time and his life for me for nothing. The preachers give up all hope of lay ing up any thing for their families, and devote themselves to trying to do good; and *do* it, I believe, whether they do me any or not. To such a man I am willing to give a part of my crop; not so small a part that I won't know it, but a good slice of my own loaf. He works for me and mine: I will work for him: it is but right. But so long as the church on this circuit has a set of official members that will not give much themselves, and key everybody else down to their own narrowness of estimate, she never will accomplish much. Why don't the Church turn such men out of office? If a man gets as happy as a camp-meeting, and only puts down five dollars, though able to give fifty, why, keep him to get happy; don't keep him to raise supplies. If a man is as rich as Crœsus, and puts down ten dollars, why, give him a ten-dollar post; don't put him in charge of an important position. Hide him out, if you can, so that the cause may not suffer from his example. If a man talks, and on this plea, or that plan, is plainly trying to reduce the whole affair of his giving to support the preacher to a point where nobody can feel it—that is, to nothing—why, out with him, if he has been in office for twenty years; for he is not fit to plan for any Church, much less to be a pillar in it. Get large-hearted men in the stewardship, and something will be done. I here give notice that I am going to move, at the fourth Quarterly Conference, if I am spared, to hustle out about one half of the old fogies in the stewardship, in order to save the preacher from starvation."

"Mr. President," said old Brother Goodsine, "I have been a quiet but by no means uninterested listener. And for the first time have I seen this matter thoroughly sifted; and I for one invoke a settled policy in our Church which will sift her Quarterly Conferences and her people. I should not go too far, sir, to say that I have prayed for it. Covetousness is 'the sin that doth so easily beset' the Methodist Church: long have I marked it. Our class-meetings and our itinerancy are our glory; our covetousness is our shame. Whatever scriptural authority there may be—and I believe there is a clearly-implied one—to exclude a member for non-attendance at class, there is a clearly-expressed authority for excluding from her pale those who are covetous-minded. It has appeared to me as the best possible evidence of covetousness that a man should feel the obligations we are under to the gospel, and yet systematically give nothing to its support. All the covetous are shut out from the city of God, as we learn from the vision of St. John, and surely they should not be retained knowingly in the Church. I have ever felt it binding on my conscience to give a tenth of my income. Abraham gave to Melchizedek a tenth out of the spoils of the five kings, long before the law; Jacob promised it, and no doubt gave it, long before; the law, which was four hundred and thirty years after, incorporated it in express terms; the Levites, who lived on tithes, were themselves required to give a tenth of their income—a tithe of tithes; and I cannot think that when the ceremonial law became of no force, this rule also passed with it, for the law, which was four hundred and thirty years after, could only leave it as an obligation where it found it. And I have asked myself, if Christ be a high-priest after the order of Melchizedek, should I not pay HIM the tithe of my income; when Abraham, and probably Jacob too, paid tithes to that priest of the most high God; first being by interpretation King of Righteousness, and after that also King of Salem—which is, King of Peace? To be safe, I have always done it, sir. For, though it may not be a part of the moral law, yet I cannot but regard it as a moral custom of the highest sanction. It is the least, sir, which a Christian man can do: so it seems to me. The gospel is a law of liberty, not that we may do the less, but the more; nor that we may use our liberty for a cloak of covetousness, but as the servants of God. These, brethren, are the thoughts and sentiments of a heart that yields to none of you in its devoted attachment to Methodism. My fear is that even from heaven I may look back with regret upon the opportunities of life for doing good which I did not, and the goods of my Lord that I used not."

The Quarterly Conference adjourned with prayer.

CHAPTER VII.

A BIG COLLECTION—ONE NOT TOO HEAVY TO "LIFT."

THE elder's plan was presented to the congregation and the church, and the list read out. The house was well filled, and, to the surprise of those who knew the habits of the squire, Brother Wallet was there. Brother Badger, whose father before him had been an assistant-treasurer of the South-Down Aid Society in England, and who regarded his office as a sort of providential reward of Providence to him, in kind, on this side of the water, was very uneasy. His plans had gone by the board, and he trembled for the fate of their author. One or two only, beside the elder, guessed the inward ferment that was going on in the old man's elements. When the quarterage notes were gathered up, and were being read out, it was found, to the surprise of the whole congregation, that Brother Badger had filled the blank with "fifty dollars." The "goats," as one of the stewards called them, came up nobly, and gave fully half as much as the church, the preacher being rather "popular." Brother Jerry, who collected the promises, it was found had forgotten to write out one for himself; and so, too, there was nothing with the squire's name to it. Hunnicut called attention to the fact by supposing that some of the notes were probably still sticking under the leather of the hat. "O!"—Jerry remembered himself, and filled out an I O U for "ten dollars." John Bear whispered to Hunnicut that there was always a long story to be told between Jerry's name and Jerry's cash.

The squire then arose, and asked liberty to say a few words about a very important matter. The elder hoped that Brother Wallet would speak: that no doubt all present would be glad to hear any thing he might please to say. The squire acknowledged the liberty in a very handsome bow, as he rather prided himself on his parts in that way, having been once told by some youngster that *he* was always reminded of the great constitutional lawyer, the great William Pinckney, whenever he saw the squire speaking in public. He proceeded to say that he had already presented a kindred suggestion to his brethren of the Quarterly Conference to the one he was about to make, to which they had but partially assented: he now offered a modified view of his original proposition. "I have been," said he, "a close and painful listener during all the sessions of the heaviest business Quarterly Conference that I have ever seen, and I hope never, my brethren, to pass through such another. Not that I will not stand with you shoulder to shoulder, but I hope it may never again be necessary." He would, he said, inform those who had not been a part of the occasion alluded to, that he had then and there spoken of a great fact—a painful fact—it was the fact that this day had witnessed—the wear, and tear, and expense to which our present imperfect system of supporting the gospel subjected us. "It is," he continued, "the duty of every man to make these burdens as light as possible. I have a financial plan, or, rather, financial discovery to make known to my fellow-citizens, by which I have estimated that the whole cost of the gospel may be reduced to a merely nominal sum*—a plan by which

* "How could our chymick friends go on
To find the philosophic stone!"—*Prior.*

——"That stone
Philosophers in vain so long have sought."
Milton.

it may support and extend itself indefinitely. Necessity has in this case proved to be the mother of invention." Two subjects had rested night and day on his mind for six years past—a greedy grave and a needy church. "In the course of my reading on the former—for," said he, "I have made it my study—I have read much about Egypt. It is a remarkable fact that most good things have come out of Egypt; and yet we have not looked to Egypt as we ought to have done for the art of burying—an art in which she stands preëminent." For it is given up, he said, that the Egyptians knew more about putting away their dead snugly, lastingly, and profitably, than all the rest of mankind put together. Their art had been lost.*

* The remarks of the squire remind one of the eloquent words of the author of Mammon: "In the early age of the Christian Church, the heavenly art of embalming property and making it immortal was not only known but practiced; but, like the process of another

He proposed that it should be restored for the benefit of the Church—to restore to the Church that which is hers by preëmption. "The great incomes," said he, "of Isis, and Osiris, and Carnac, were from the dead. Let us, then, learn a lesson from the Egyptians, and put the Church on her ancient financial legs once more." He regarded embalming as the perfection of the art of burying, and ants in resin as the perfection of that art. It was the great scriptural method: Joseph, it would be remembered,

---

embalming, it has now, for ages, been practically lost. Not that its principles have been unknown: these have always presented themselves on the page of truth in lines of living light. But, though benevolence has never been unknown as a theory, the perverting influence of a worldly spirit has been rendering it more and more impracticable as an art. So that now, when the obvious application of its principles is pointed out, and the necessity of carrying these principles into practice is daily becoming more urgent, we begin to be aware of the vast distance to which the Church has been drifted from the course of its duty by the current of the world, and how difficult it will be to effect a return."

was embalmed. Three miles from Rome are the catacombs, where they buried the martyrs—subterraneous cavities visited to this day with devotion—there the primitive Christians assembled themselves for worship. The sandy soil of Lybia and the countries about Egypt indicate, at one time, a large growth of pine. He doubted not that the bitumen with which the dead were saturated was that known to us by the name of resin. "Here," said he, holding up a piece of resin, with a death-watch ("hominy-beater") in it, "you can see for yourselves: pass it round. Yes, this great problem I believe to be at last solved.* But I go farther: I say we

---

* That which was an extravagance of the squire's imagination in 1850, became a fact in 1856; so great is human progress! The following was clipped from a New Orleans Daily, of June 30th:

"EMBALMING THE DEAD.—P. CASANAVE, Undertaker, No. 37 Marias street, between Custom-house and Bienville, having purchased a right from Dr. Holmes, of New York city, of EMBALMING THE DEAD, will attend

may have our own catacombs. Let us, for instance, have under our churches crypts or cellars set apart, as in the old country, to the preservation of our dead. Let it be a monopoly of the Church. Let these enormous expenses of burial be no longer diverted from their lawful and ancient channels. But, [looking at Hunnicut,] some may be ready to ask, 'Would *you* embalm all *your* dead in this way, provided the Church should adopt it?' I am ready to say at a word, I would; though, as I give the art, I could

---

promptly to all orders, by day or night. The process is simple, and is done with no inconvenience or exposure. Bodies embalmed by him are warranted to keep free from decomposition, and can be taken to any part of the world without exhaling the slightest odor, in any season of the year. Bodies in an advanced state of decomposition restored to a perfect state of preservation. Full particulars in pamphlets will be given to those who may apply.—N. B. Deceased ministers, physicians, and lawyers, will be embalmed free of charge."

Why *lawyers* should be embalmed free of charge is matter for deep reflection!

not in that case agree to find the resin. Besides, I have my own little patch of graves, that ought of right to be first filled out. Still, I am ready to say this: if I had but the half of what I lost in '48 of cholera, I would be more than glad to embalm the rest of them, and find the resin myself."

"Well, Squire Wallet," said Brother Oakhart, "you find the catacombs, and Clay here and I—we'll keep the church in *rosum*."

Brother Jake Bellus said that, for his part, he was afraid of so much *rosum* in the church: it was healthy, but he thought it was dangerous.

Brother Sam Bellus said that he did not agree with his brother: *he* was not afraid of the "rosum," but he was scared at having those catacombs about.

During the excitement or rather sensation produced by the squire's speech—which is rather to be set down to a desperate state of mind, superinduced by constant charity, or, what is the same thing, by constant calls for the support of the Church, and which sought a temporary relief in the most desperate propositions—Hunnicut slipped up and obtained from the squire his note for "ten dollars."

It was found that Brother Goodsine had given a note for seventy-five dollars; and so, too, John Bear exceeded his apportionment to the same amount. Sister Hardiman also went above hers, the depth of her poverty abounding to her liberality. Several of the official members went below their apportionment: the most of them, however, to the surprise of themselves as well as of others, actually stood it. The Brothers Bellus, after a great deal of whispering and shaking of heads, went a trifle below the mark, which was most likely owing to some misconception as to what was expected.

"The stewards of the other societies in the circuit will now," said the elder. "take this apportionment-list to their societies, and read it at their next appointments, as we have here, and pursue the same course. Take notes. I will furnish the blanks. Brother Goodsine will please attend at the next appointment at Postville, and, as far as possible, at the other preaching-places, to aid the resident stewards in bringing this plan before the people. It is rather too much to expect of the preacher in charge that he shall present and urge a plan that is mainly for his own benefit; and our system does not contemplate that he shall do it."

One of the brethren from Crane's said that he hoped the elder would appoint Brother Jerry Larkum to go along with them, and give them a lift; that somehow, or somehow else, Brother Jerry had a monstrous hold upon the people down his way.

A "Flat" brother said he was just going to ask the same thing; that this was a new thing, in the start like, and he would like to have things go off brash as possible.

The elder replied, "Y-e-s," rather slowly, that if brethren requested it, he supposed that Brother Larkum could assist in the matter. It was evident that in truth he did not at first relish the proposition of having his plan marred by Jerry's inaugurating it. But in a moment it occurred to him that possibly there were some who could be more effectually reached by Jerry than by any other type of character; and that, most likely, Brother Goodsine would bring up the last of the column, and prevent a defeat.

Jerry said that so far as any thing lay in him, he was willing to lay himself out to carry out the elder's big plan; that he believed that if any thing could make a crab-apple tree grow golden pippins, it was this guano-plan the elder had given them such a fact-insight to.

While the brothers Bellus were evidently consulting on some equally important movement, Hunnicut said that he would be happy to have the brothers Bellus come over to Hunnicut's, and help in the matter, as Brother Bear and he intended to be at "Bellus's" at the next appointment. This arrangement gave mutual satisfaction.

It was ascertained that the quarterage notes given at the quarterly meeting amounted to more than eight hundred dollars, which led the elder to remark that he had long been convinced that our people only needed to have *clearly stated* what was to be done, and what share was expected of each person; that the stewards should see to this; that unless the whole amount of expense for the year was known, and also the highest and the lowest item apportioned, an individual could not know his comparative duty. He believed that the plan of apportioning would work this year: if not perfectly this, yet it would the next; that if the stewards kept to it, it would soon become *public opinion* that a Church-member ought to give the amount apportioned to him, or have a good reason for not doing it; that whatever persons gave from time to time, could be marked on the back of their notes; that, as expenses were going on all the time, it would be more convenient possibly for members and preacher to pay quarterly; or if to the class-leader weekly, the sum would be credited on the class-book, and reported and credited on the notes at each Quarterly Conference.

After which was sung the hymn,

> "Lord, dismiss us with thy blessing,
> Bid us now depart in peace;
> Still on heavenly manna feeding,
> Let our faith and love increase."

The benediction followed.

Thus ended what was always called by certain of the brethren of Post-Oak, "The great quarterly meeting—you know, where we did so much business."

CHAPTER VIII.

THE VERY LAST DAYS—THE DAYS OF THE LAST COLLECTION.

WHILE the congregation was going out, it was arrested by the entry of three gentlemen, one of whom, the First Elder of the First Church of Oakville, called out and requested friends to come back and be seated for a moment. He then proceeded to say that it would be recollected that the First Church had called, some twelve months ago, the Rev. Zelophehad Crane to be its settled pastor; but that, owing to the great unwillingness the congregation at Lynn, Massachusetts, had manifested to the severing of the pastoral relations which existed between it and its beloved pastor, the call had not been accepted; that the First Church had persisted, and had made the call considerably more urgent; but the Lynn congregation continued unyielding; that, at two several times thereafter, the First Church increased the call by twenty-five and thirty-three per cent., the Lynn congregation continuing impracticably indisposed to part with its able pastor; that, indeed, at two subsequent times, the First Church swelled the call by fifty and seventy-five per cent.; but the congregation at Lynn would not break its hold upon its highly popular pastor. At length the First Church doubled the original call; and he was happy to have it to say that the congregation at Lynn was compelled, as it were, to give its reluctant consent to the dissolution of its hitherto existing pastoral relations with its distinguished pastor. Brother Crane had arrived several Sabbaths ago, and wished to give out a notice.

The reverend gentleman stepped forward into the altar, being about thirty, tall, pale, and bronchially disposed to a good deal of hair under the throat.

"If you be patient, dear friends of Oakville," said he, "for a few brief moments, we will, not to define more accurately the contingent providences which have so unexpectedly brought us, through two-thirds of the entire length of the Valley of the Mississippi, to this much-neglected waste, indulge in a few remarks. And, firstly:

"IN REGARD TO OURSELF.

"We are the seventh son of Zebra Crane, a name less universally known, perhaps, than that of either of his sons. The entire seven were set apart from childhood by our father to the Valley of the Mississippi, to carry light to them that sit in that Valley; even to them that dwell in its extreme south-west region, and Texas. And it is a singular corroborative existing providence, that all of us are just now in the one calling. It is desired, perhaps, that we state further: Our eldest brother, the Rev. Zeba Crane, is a graduate of the North-by-East Theological School. The second son, the Rev. Zalmunna, is a graduate of the East-by-North Theological Seminary. The third, the Rev. Zeboim, is a graduate of the North-East-by-North Theological College. The fourth, the Rev. Zadok, is a graduate of the North-North-East Theological Institute. The fifth, the Rev. Zerah, is a graduate of the North-East Theological Academy. The sixth, the Rev. Zebulun, is a graduate of the North-East-by-East Theological Institution. The seventh, Ze, or Zed, or, as you of the South-west call it, Izzard, is a regular graduate of the East-North-East Theological Collegiate Institute: that is ourself.

"Secondly:

"THE SPIRIT IN WHICH WE ARE COME.

"We are here, dear friends, in the spirit of an exhaustless subjective religious earnest-mindedness, and in the progressive development of a consuming objective zeal.

"Thirdly:

"OUR COURSES OF SERIAL LECTURES.

"We shall resume our serial treatment of the great objective interests which present themselves immediately to our religious consciousness, as follows:

"On Sabbath evening next: our Second Serial Lecture to Young Men—their Wants and Ways. And on the evening of the Lord's day, next thereafter, our Third Serial Lecture to Young Men—their Singular and Providential Adaptation to the Wants of the Present Times; also, with Closing Remarks to their Surviving Parents. Young ladies as well as young men should not fail to attend, *en masse*, each one of this Series of Lectures.

"On Monday evening next, our First Serial Lecture of a Course on the Recent Flight or Hegira of the Pope to Gaeta; the Military Occupation of Armageddon; the Fall of Babylon; and the Solution of the hitherto painful Mystery of the Objective Number Six Hundred and Sixty-six.

"On Tuesday evening, our Second Serial Lecture of a Course on the Recognition of Friends in a Future State.

"On Wednesday evening, our First Serial Lecture of a Course on the Valley of the Mississippi; its unparalleled destitution: concluding with a Bird's-eye View of the Moral Misery of the Great South-west, and Texas.

"On Thursday evening, *Deo Volente*, our First Serial Discussion of a Course upon the Ethnographical Traces of the Probable Whereabouts of the Ten Lost Tribes.

"On Friday evening, we would also give notice that, in place of our intended Lecture on the Immortality of Thought in connection with Mind, there will be a Lecture delivered in the First Church, by the Reverend Visiting Brother to our right—Rabbi Simeon Ben Bone, a converted Israelite of the tribe of Judah, the Travelling Secretary of the Hebrew Ways and Means Society of New York—on the Destructive Elements which have surrounded, and the Antiseptic Qualities which have preserved, the Israelites; their present Atomic State, and the Providential Affinities which are likely to result in their speedy Reünion, and their National Restoration to the Skies of their Native Judea.

"On Saturday evening, our last Lecture for the week, and our First Serial of a Course on the Waldenses; with remarks upon the Albigenses, the Vaudois, and the present painful politico-papistical persecutions prevalent in Piedmont.

"These Lectures are without charge, dear friends, excepting that on Friday evening. Our converted Brother, Rabbi Ben Bone, is making a collection for the Last Days. He feels that the time is short; and the elders of the First Church consent that he shall realize, for the expenses of that eventful period, a Last Collection."

At this personal allusion, the Reverend Ben Bone, who was short, hearty, and whiskered, bowed assent, and rolled his eyes beneath his specs, as if the time had come, and he were going under. However, he became immediately conscious of his mission and himself, and rose with an auctioneer air: "Dat ish true, gentleman and ladish, it ish de very last day. I make haste—Judah vill no more vex Ephram. Dis ish dat vat I say, so as de shervant of Abram, she shpake to Laban, Give me vat I vant quick, and so you let me go—eh? vat you say?"

The squire had arisen. He bowed, and

said that he arose merely to ask a question; that the restoration of Israel, more particularly Judah, was a subject of great interest to him, associated as it was in his mind with the exhumation of Nineveh and the drying up of the Dead Sea; that he had always indulged in the reflection that that first great act of the last great drama would be attended with no outlay or expense to the Gentile branch of the Church. He had imagined that the outcasts of Israel, more particularly Judah, would, in the main, return to their native Judea, singing, on foot. Did he understand the Reverend Doctor Bonebone aright—that the Church would be, in fact was now, called upon to defray the expense of the restoration? As to feeling interest, he might say a prayerful interest, in the millennium, he yielded to none present. He trusted it *had* at last come. "O," said he, looking somewhat rapt, "whenever my mind looks that way, I instinctively cry out with the poet:

"Happy, happy day!
When the King himself shall say
To all the Church:
'The poor heathen's way
From earth to heaven,
You need no longer pay,
Nor for them search:
They have arriven.'"

"Dat ish so imposhible as it can be," replied the Doctor, warmly. "I hab shurveyed de whole routes by mine ownshelf; and dare ish rubbish, rubbish enough. Vat for dat you tink de shcattered of Judah she comb back on bare foots! I tell you she ride on de backs of kings, mit de shteamvistle and de frigat of shteams. De Gentiles, she musht pay de whole of all de exhpenshe. De time ish comb. You gives me nothinks: I gives you no shtocks in de New Yerushalam."

The squire rejoined, bowing, that if that were the case, he should, at the earliest moment, attentively review the views of those commentators who favor the doctrine of a *spiritual* restoration of Israel, more particularly Judah.

When the brothers Bellus turned their horses' heads toward home, there began a conversation, or, more properly speaking, a discussion, which was continued at intervals for three months. It was a Monday morning. During the night there had fallen a fine shower of rain; and as they were early on the road, their senses were greeted with the freshly-washed forest leaves, hanging like emeralds in the morning sun, and with the cheerful note of the woodlark, as it filled and rung through the woodland. To all which the brothers were insensible, for things had transpired during their visit at Oakville which furnished the ride home with subject-matter of endless speculation: Quarterly Conference, and all that; then the high learning of Parson Crane, and of all the Cranes; the "lectures;" the "skeery times' which were coming; the "last days," which had come; and the "visiting brother," whc had come with them. "Brother Jake," said Sam, "I have studied over it, but I can't somehow make it come up clear to me, about the First Church. You see the providence of the thing was on their side. That's clear. But the cross-providence behind that is what gets me. I can see it clear enough in a skim like on the top, but then it runs off into a fog, a deep fog. The 'Lynn congregation' was against providence. That's clear; though I don't think there was any providence in the Lynn congregation on the congregation side. The 'First Church' side was the providence side; but it was a strong pull first. And that is what gets me again, because providence, you see, always does pull strong; that is, when she pulls her own pulling; and if she had not pulled mighty strong, the First Church could not have got hold of Parson Crane at all—of course it could not. I am clear on that providence. But I am not so clear on the First Church: I wish I was."

"I can't see it clear as you see it, Brother Sam," replied Jake. "You see, providence is a mighty ticklish sort of thing to see into; for it runs into a curlikew, and then into fine ravelings, and then fetches you up to a dead stand. I am clear on the First Church getting Parson Crane—that it was a clear providence, sure enough. But the deep providence was, the hold that the Lynn congregation had on him. Then it begins: one providence sets against another providence, and this providence devours up that other providence, and breaks the hold of the Lynn congregation, which was the greatest providence of all."

"You see, Brother Jake," returned Sam, "the greatest of all the providences was the providence on the side of Parson Crane, because it got him out of the Lynn congregation, and set him down in the First Church."

"Very like," said Jake; "I grant you, Brother Sam, it was the greatest, sure enough, but not the clearest greatest. It seems to me that the First Church was a ladder of providence, and Parson Crane climbed on it out of the Lynn congregation; or else the Lynn congregation was a ladder, and Parson Crane climbed up on it into the First Church; and the more I study on which side the providence of it lay, the less clear it comes up to me."*

---

* Was this style formed upon that of any of the classics? Apart from the labor which this supposition would imply, the rare coincidence of equal success in the case of two brothers precludes such a solution of the matter. Yet it must have occurred to the reader that Plato was never more like himself than "the two" are like him: of course we speak only of style. A few sentences from the *Parmenides*, (26,) which are subjoined, will serve to verify the impressions of the reader. The whole is interesting, as one of those freaks of nature where the speech of the uneducated equals that of the best models; and shows that the quality "*sapientiæ insanientis*" is one of the possibilities of a truly great mind:—

'Being different from itself, it would surely be different from 'one,' and so would not be one. True. And if it should be the same with different, it would be that, ('different,') and would not be itself; so that 'one' would thus be not what it is, but different from 'one.' It would not indeed. It will then be not the same with 'different,' or different from itself? It will not. But it will not be different from 'different' while it is 'one.' For it does not belong to 'one' to be different from any thing, but to be 'different' alone, and to nothing else. Right. In consequence, then, of its being 'one,' it will not be 'different;' or do you think (it can?) Certainly not;" etc., etc.—*Parmenides of Plato*, 26—*by G. Burgess*.

CHAPTER IX.

THE GLORIOUS ECONOMY OF A MILLENNIUM.

On his way home from the adjoining circuit, the presiding elder preached again at Oakville. It was on a week-day, and the house was well filled. The text was, "And take heed to yourselves, lest at any time your hearts be overcharged with surfeiting, and drunkenness, and cares of this life, and so that day come upon you unawares. For as a snare shall it come on all them that dwell on the face of the whole earth. Watch ye therefore, and pray always, that ye may be accounted worthy to escape all these things that shall come to pass, and to stand before the Son of man." Luke xxi. 34–36.

It was an address which carried conviction to the consciences of his hearers: a kind of preaching which cannot be very exactly reported, on account of its effect upon the reporter. A few passages were secured. "It is feared by some," said the preacher, "that the time for missionary zeal is not yet; that we may possibly be found too fast; that a better state of things, it may be, will soon set in—a prophecy of Joel, a Millennium, a large measure of saving power, of light and love, which will save the nations without being much of a drain upon the Church, requiring few men and no money.* And this view is important in the respect of the drain; and glorious enough, but only in that respect. The agencies of the

* "All exterior property is doomed to be consumed at the last day: it is desirable that as much of it as possible should have been as long as possible put in such employments as will produce results that will not suffer by the *last* fire."—*John Foster*.

present Dispensation are sufficient to give the world the gospel. The reign of grace abounds wherever sin has abounded, and that is everywhere; and much more abounds. The Church has in the Holy Spirit an agent as effective for good as was the Saviour on earth; for Christ since then has become a High Priest for men, at the throne; the Holy Spirit does not confine himself to place, as Jesus, who ministered only to the circle around his person.

"The defect of this Dispensation, if it has one, is the amount of self-denial that is essential to the working of the present gospel agency. Any arrangement which would let off the Church from its share of this labor of love might be considered an improvement upon the present gospel, and might be considered millennial by just so much as it rendered self-denial superfluous. In which case there would be the development of a spirit quite different from that which constrained the apostle to approve himself a minister of God in much patience, in afflictions, in necessities, in distresses.

"To 'work while it is day' is the teaching of Christ. The present Dispensation may end unexpectedly; so the Church is exhorted to be sober and watch unto prayer—'Behold the Bridegroom cometh!' Then will the day end. Then shall set in a time of sight rather than of faith, a time of judicial rigor, a time when every tongue shall confess and every knee bend, though not by persuasion. The storm-cloud upon the horizon warns the husbandman to gather in his grain. In those days mercy will not rejoice against judgment. Then it will be too late for foolish virgins to get oil in their vessels: they may seek it, but the door will be shut. That which once answered the purpose, will no longer avail. 'Then shall they call upon me, but I will not answer.' 'When once the master of the house has risen up and shut to the door, many shall seek to enter in, but shall not be able.' In vain shall they cry, 'Lord, Lord, open unto us,' when this Dispensation shall have ended. Thus the Saviour enforces *present* activity.

Between the golden age of prophecy and this present day, there is a period in which the air is so filled with falling fragments of heaven and earth, with blood, and fire, and vapor of smoke, that one cannot see the new fields and skies where righteousness is to dwell. When the mediatorial day shall have passed, and the judicial shall have set in, then shall the souls under the altar cry as Abel's blood, and be heard. Then shall those who survive that time of trial be especially honored. The Church, in those days of perplexity, shall triumph through great tribulation. 'To him that overcometh will I give to eat of the tree of life that is in the midst of the paradise of God.'

"This present Dispensation is a day of

mercy—of change from bad to good—to a world of sinners a day of grace; but not that day: 'When the righteous be scarcely saved, where will the ungodly and the sinner appear?' Now, Christ calls sinners to repentance; then, he shall call the righteous to judgment: 'Gather my saints together unto me—for God is judge himself.' The Church is warned by Christ to improve the present, as a man should his life, for it must end. Yet many are waiting, waiting for the Millennium! They are reading books which render, through their adroit interpretation of the prophets, the work of saving men from death a matter just about to be accomplished by the personal reign of Christ, without cost! The Church groans under the privilege she has of laboring, with Christ, in the saving of a world. Her deliverance draweth nigh, when she will be called neither to suffer nor to reign with him. Brethren, this is the time for action.

Imitate Him who *worked* while it was day. For the end cometh: 'these be the days of vengeance:' when no man can work. Behold! now is the acceptable day of the Lord; and now you may be saviours of men. In that day when the Father shall visibly exalt Him who humbled himself, may you be found worthy to stand in the presence of the King in his glory!"

CHAPTER X.

SOME GAMMON, BUT MORE GRAPE.

In due course of time the meeting was held at Postville. Brother Goodsine was there, and successful in his presentation of the plan. The people went far beyond any thing that had been in preceding times given at that place. In his speech he quoted the language of the great Chalmers against covetousness: "The disease is as near to universal as it is virulent. Wealth is the goddess whom all the world worshippeth. There is many a city in our empire, of which, with an eye of apostolical discernment, it may be seen that it is wholly given over to idolatry." He dwelt at length upon his view, that the gospel does not release from the obligation to devote a portion of our property to God; that there was no legal obligation upon Abraham or upon Jacob to pay tithes; that they did it, but did it from motives that should actuate every Christian at the present day. It was a thank-offering unto Almighty God, an acknowledgment of dependence upon him, and of his mercy in the bestowment of temporal blessings. There is a covenant to which we should become a party by the payment of a tenth of our yearly income; that we may obtain that favor of God upon the labor of our hands which alone can secure us against want, or make our plenty a blessing to our children and ourselves. This was, Jacob's vow at Bethel: "If God will be with me and will keep me in this way that I go, and will give me bread to eat and raiment to put on, so that I come again to my father's house in peace: then shall the Lord be my God; and this stone which I have set up for a pillar shall be God's house; and of all that thou shalt give me I will surely give the tenth unto thee." "What was the result of this youthful vow?" continued the old man; "hear it, my brethren: let Jacob, in the height of his manhood and at the high-tide of a prosperous life, tell it: 'With my staff I passed over this Jordan, and now I am become two bands.' Hear him reäffirm it, when his eyes were 'dim for age so that he could not see,' blessing his grandsons in the name of 'the God of Abraham and Isaac, the God which fed me all my life long unto this day.' Let us confess our sin. Let us no more refuse to bring into the house of God our tithes and offerings. The times of this ignorance God winked at, but now commandeth all of us to repent. The effectual doors which are open in our own country and in heathendom demand liberal men, and make the love of money in the Church a sin of great enormity in the sight of God. Unless we set apart no mean portion of our income, how shall we do our duty to the poor, as well as to the gospel? Shall we be able to say, in the day of affliction, when the actions of a past life pass in review, 'If I have withheld the poor from their desire, or have caused the eyes of the widow to fail; or if I have eaten my morsel myself alone, and the fatherless hath not eaten thereof; if I have seen any perish for want of clothing, or any poor without covering; if his loins have not blessed me, and if he were not warmed with the fleece of my sheep; then let mine arm fall from my shoulder-blade.' We must give largely out of our income without reference to the increase of our property. Happiness and virtue go together, and they are as frequently found in company with an humble fortune as with a large one."

There must have been a great time at

Crane's School-house, from the wonderful account which brethren from that region gave afterwards of "Brother Jerry's great juniper-talk:"—"But he himself went a day's journey into the wilderness, and came and sat down under a juniper tree." 1 Kings xix. 4.

"I wonder!" replied one, who had to regret it all his after-life that he was not there. He was afraid, he said, "from the reports that came down, that some new kilter was agoing to be started;" and, for his part, he did not want to be there during any such doings; but if he had known that "Brother Jerry was agoing to take on so high, why, of course," said he, "I should not have missed it for any thing."

"Well now, he did," said the informer; "if he didn't, nobody ever did."

"I wonder!" exclaimed the absentee.

"Brother Jerry," continued the informer, "argued and argued until no man could tell whither from which, and just walked over every thing. My! he fairly spread himself when he came to talk about the fire, and the angel gathering juniper-chips to cook an ash-cake for a poor travelling preacher. You could have heard a pin drop. Then, when he came to the king sitting at home in plenty and purple—Georgium sidus! how he cavorted—well he did!"

"I declare!" exclaimed the now thoroughly wretched absentee. "I was a great fool to miss such a chance. If it had not been for the old woman, somehow I think I should have been there; but she sort of skeered me about them money doings."

The informer could have had no pity upon the poor absentee, for he continued: "And when Jerry came to the earthquake there, Yes, says he, nothing can move you; it takes a whole earthquake of justice these days to move a three-legged stool. And when all the elements are roaring and wrestling and whistling and rolling in their fury-pitch, and every thing around is snapping, why, then, says he, you just come to the door and ask if any thing is to pay! No, says he, nothing can melt you. When you have been in a blast-furnace, with wind and fire playing on you for years together, enough to melt rocks, you don't spill as much silver, says he, as would solder up a drop-leak in a tin pail, if it fell square on the spot: when, says he, the very moment you drop into the black lake, the silver that's on you will sink you like a dead body with a stone sewed up in a bag. My! when he said that! Why, says he, don't you stir yourselves to do mercy? But you say, 'O, I am so religious! there is no one about here that has religion like me!' I am sorry to say, says Jerry, there are a plenty left just as religious as you. If you know your duty and you won't do it, says he, I tell you now, it's a gone fawn-skin, as sure as you are born."

"Well," asked the absentee, "you say he did get right smart: did Brother Jerry pay any thing himself?"

"O yes," replied the informer, "certainly he did; for he told us he was not only giving us his exhortation, but throwing in his quarterage note besides. Jerry told us he wanted no more dime collections: that day had gone by; so most everybody signed for five or ten dollars."

From all accounts, Jerry was a better hand at enforcing a duty than he was at discharging it. He gave them another powerful time at the Flats—on the thumbs and great-toes of Adoni-bezek: "But Adoni-bezek fled; and they pursued after him, and caught him, and cut off his thumbs and his great-toes." Judges i. 6. So that it was a disputed point between a few from the Flats and an equal number from Crane's which was the greater, his 'great juniper-talk' or his 'great big-toe talk;' and as each party heard only the one talk, it is likely to remain an open question. An old sister very properly observed of the latter, that she had never heard that text run that way before. His propositions were :

I. Without great-toes and thumbs no man could work or travel. Money was the great-toes and thumbs of every travelling-preacher. It was the great-toes and thumbs of every Church, and of every Missionary Society.

II. The man who did not give his money to support the gospel, cut off the great-toes and thumbs of the gospel ministry and the gospel Church.

III. That if any man kept at it, maiming and laming, right and left, making ministers and missionaries—gospel kings—gather meat under his table, and then in fact give them no meat to gather, that very soon he should be overtaken, caught, and fixed himself for slow travelling ; he should be worm-cropt and sheriff-sheared of all his thumbs and all his great-toes, real and personal, and should have "ADONI-BEZEK" written on his forehead, read and known of all men. He warned them that no man could outrun an army-worm or a boll-worm, or a fire, or a freeze, or the cholera; and unless a man could do that, he had better do his duty, and save his crop—that he himself felt in duty bound to save his own great-toes and thumbs by signing up.

The fact was about as the elder had surmised. There were some at these appointments who could be reached by Jerry, but not a few others who could only be induced to come into the new method by a very different kind of approach.

Brother Goodsine visited the appointment several weeks later, and gave them one of his unpretending, earnest appeals. After stating the plan, he gave a history of the failure of every former year in their effort to support a preacher, and then enforced upon them their duty as members of that circuit and of the Church of the New Testament. "O for a race of men," said he, "who shall devote all their earnings to the cause of Christ, reserving only enough for the comfortable sustenance of themselves and their dependents! O for a race of merchants, shipmasters, mechanics, of artists, of farmers, lawyers, employers and employés, who will devote themselves to God as much as if they were ministers! thus raising the common employments of life to the sublime dignity of preaching the gospel. Many a man is called to this entire devotion of the ordinary business of his life; but, supposing that a useful and an entire devotion can only be in the calling of a preacher, he has left the sphere where he might have been eminently useful to the cause of Christ, by giving the fruit of his skill and industry, for a sphere that God never intended to be his. Devoted hands are at this day wanted as well as tongues. Devoted fortunes, devoted energetic business men, are the pressing need of the Church of Christ. They are all that our own Methodism requires to make her the most efficient Church since the days of Paul. 'The legs of the lame are not equal,' says Solomon; and a Church may possess a devoted ministry, but if she has not a devoted membership, she will go forth lamely upon all her enterprises of mercy. The ministers of our Church need the backing of an energetic, consecrated, zealous membership. Ready to go forth to the ends of the earth, will you send them? Ready to work to the end of life, will you support them? Will you let them die in the harness of battle? Will you cease not to care for the mother and the babes, who share their toil and poverty? May my right hand forget its cunning if I discharge not these obligations to the utmost!"

"The Belluses'" was a point of considerable interest. It was a large and rather poor congregation. Here the two brothers were very influential, and they entered into the new method very heartily. On the appointed day, Hunnicut and John Bear were present. Hunnicut had insisted that no one should be called out until "the two" had spoken: that they could make the whole matter plainer and present it more forcibly to their brethren than any other men in the State, or probably in the world.

Brother Sam said, he did not know, but perhaps it was so somewhat.

Brother Jake said that he knew it was so, but he thought that perhaps it might like as not be some other way too.

After a short sermon by the preacher in charge, the congregation was detained, and Brother Sam was called upon to explain the new plan of the stewards. He said, he did not know, but he supposed that the most of them had heard of the big quarterly meeting that had just a few weeks gone been held at

Oakville. He was there: He had read of meetings of politics, and meetings of associations, and meetings of camp-meetings, and had seen somewhat thereof of them, but such a meeting as that was, he had never seen, or heard of, or read of, such a sort. He had seen the stewards at a stand, the leaders at a stand, Brother Badger at a stand, Brother Jerry at a stand, himself at a stand, and Brother Jake here at a dead stand; "and there we stood and stood. Well, brethren, says the elder, now for your plans, brush up. Brother Jake and I, we *could not* think." Just here Jake, who was in the altar, stepped forward, and Sam fell back a step, listening very particularly. Brother Jake said, No, not that: he could think, but could not have said a word if you had offered a township. He saw where things was; and one plan came up, and another plan came up, and they chased each other and tumbled and rolled over and over in his head like two kittens, until they got his head in a whirligig, so that he could not have spoken so his own dog "Brutus" would have known him; and he naturally sat still. But when Squire Wallet wanted to bury one half the membership with cholera, to pay the expenses of the gospel on the other half; and then the Church was to turn round and bury free-gratis for nothing as many of the squire's hands as chose to lay down and die—"And where should we have all been if *that* plan had been voted? Sure enough, head deep in debt. Brother Sam he was not against the debt so much as I."

"No," interposed Sam, "I was not against the debt so much as the sickness. I really thought once it was going to carry. The squire is a mighty strong speaker, and they say the squire will get a large vote this summer. But I could not sit still. I spoke and Jake spoke. The squire sort of backed out. Next day at it again. Then I spoke up: I said, it was dangerous to have *rosum* about a church. The squire wanted the underneath of every meeting-house full of rosummated corpses. I said it would not work; so *that* plan was spoiled. Brother Jake here, he did not mind the rosum."

"I did not for true," said Jake, "mind the rosum, so much as I did them catacoombs —that was *another* plan of the squire's. I knew we down here could not stand to have them things about."

So they went on. Hunnicut reported their speeches, and no doubt colored them highly with his own humor. He states that, at times, no one on earth could have understood them but that particular society; every thing, however, seemed to it clear and highly satisfactory, though Brother Bear and himself had to go out and see after their horses more than once, to keep from being convulsed.

The more exact account of the matter is,

the audience was one accustomed to the honest simplicity of the two brothers, who bore excellent characters as good men, good neighbors, and good planters; and, by an intimate acquaintance with them and their families, it could justly appreciate the qualities which lay behind their unique efforts in public at intelligible speech.

"The two" succeeded in showing that the new method was an escape from other dreaded ones, and so took "the scare," which they had so emphatically deprecated in the Quarterly Conference, completely out of the congregation.

CHAPTER XI.

"CHARITY WHICH NEVER FAILETH."

THE friend who was so kind as to furnish a report of Brother Goodsine's speech at "Crane's," may be recognized by the public when we inform them that he is the large and frequent donor to the Missionary Society of the Methodist Church, and to the American Bible Society, who signs himself "PANOLA." The reader will certainly pardon a fuller introduction to friend P.

On every Sabbath morning, just before church-time, he may be seen at —— Chapel, a fresh-looking, neatly-dressed gentleman of middle age and stature. His hat, which is still on, is of white wool, broad-rimmed and of good quality; his clothes of a light drab. He has regular features, a large hazel eye, a well-formed, rather full person. "I wish you a good-morning, young ladies, young gentlemen, friends: this is a beautiful Sabbath." While he is speaking, several cotton-wagons drive round to the church, filled with women and children from his plantation: their faces are shining with the blandness which the negro wears on his way to Sunday-church; their clothes are white as meal, and their head-kerchiefs are bright as hawberries and jessamine.

Friend P. had inherited, while young, a fine property from his father; but having endorsed largely for "friends," had, in very few years after attaining his majority, to part with both his servants and plantation. His uncle became the purchaser of both, and thus saved him the pain of seeing family servants sold to strangers. Upon this reverse, he found a living in the toilsome business of teaching. His wife then proved herself to be, as he says, a wife from the Lord. Though brought up in Southern ease and affluence, she applied herself to teaching with him, and often told her husband that she was happier than ever. During this period of their history, they were both converted, at a protracted-meeting on the Panola Circuit—a circuit, by-the-by, a long way from Post-Oak. Seven years after his reverse, the uncle, who had amassed a large property by rigid economy and continual cotton-planting, died, having devised to his nephew all the estate he had purchased of him, and one-half of the remainder of his own property to his nephew's wife. A year or two after this unlooked-for fortune, the typhoid fever appeared in the neighborhood of their plantation: their servants were nearly all attacked with it. For several months the master and mistress were nursing and waiting night and day, until both of them were brought to death's verge with an attack of the same disease. Being advised to aid a very slow recovery with a sea-voyage, it ended in their making a trip to Europe. On their way back, through Germany, friend P. fell in with a settlement of Moravians, and became greatly impressed with their zeal for missions. Upon his return home, he dedicated his yearly income to the spread of the gospel, and himself to doing good. He has long since been known by all the poor in his neighborhood, and loved by all the children. The people and preachers of Panola Circuit speak of him as a model of a church-steward.

Every Sabbath afternoon he teaches a Bible-class, in which he has gathered nearly all the young people of the settlement. He has in his study a choice library; and almost always he has one or two poor young men at "the Ridge," whom he is teaching in the higher parts of an education. Several missionaries are in the far East who received from him no ordinary fin sh; and whose zeal for the cause of Christ consumes daily, in labors "more abundant," all the powers with which they are daily supplied.

When it is added that friend P. and his wife are blessed with two children, a son and a daughter, both of whom are about grown, and very like their parents in person and disposition, the reader will have a single-line picture of one of the noblest of Southern planters.

Hearing that he was at Crane's when Brother Goodsine presented the plan, we requested, upon the liberty of an old acquaintance, a report of the old man's speech, and added a request for a paper upon Christian beneficence; stating, at the same time, what we purposed to publish of the history of Post-Oak. The paper we insert just as it came to hand, in the body of his letter, even at the risk of interrupting the connection between Post-Oak and the mind of the reader:

PANOLA RIDGE.

MY DEAR BROTHER:

You will find with this an imperfect report of Mr. Goodsine's speech. My being at Crane's School-house was, as you supposed, an accident. And a very agreeable surprise to me it was, to find a body of Methodists accomplishing what we had been so long talking of on our own circuit.

Mr. Goodsine's speech was impressive, and, I should judge, quite effective. The value of the tithe argument for enforcing the obligation of a Christian to give, had never been justly appreciated by me. He convinced me that Christian obligation stands upon this basis, though Christian benevolence rests upon a better. The tithe-quantity is the limit in one direction: the only limit in the other is, all you are and have. He presented to my mind the "power" which would characterize a Church whose membership measured up to the Levitical standard of liberality, so that I could but wish Methodism were more Levitical in the measure of her thank-offerings. The financial plan which he presented seemed to be a good working method for collecting equitably the expenses of a circuit. But the tithe system, it occurred to me, would be the better prescription for both circuit and Church.

Galvanic remedies have been the settled treatment for the chronic financial ailments of our Church. And the labors of a self-sacrificing ministry have proved adequate thus far to periodically electrify the membership into the discharge of a part of their duty. This at best secures but an occasional, uncertain, and unreliable action. The difference between it and vital motion of mercy is very great. Like the stupor which precedes death from Arctic cold, the deadly slumber of a soul chilled by covetousness is creeping over our Church, and the most exciting and incessant efforts barely suffice to arrest the fatal torpor. Methodism is like a person whose entire right side is paralyzed. The cause of Missions suffers paralysis. The cause of Education moves only by the large sacrifices of a few; while the labor of securing a sum sufficient to build a church has come to be so great, that the most zealous become worn-out and disheartened by a few successful efforts.

The support of the ministry is meagre, and the annual deficiencies so great, that it is questionable if they, as a class, do not mainly support the gospel. The families of deceased ministers are so poorly cared for, that the conviction must often be forced upon them that the Methodists are incapable of common gratitude. In raising the current expenses of a church, the membership have again and again to be approached, urged, and coaxed into the most ordinary contribution toward the support of the gospel. When ministers have worn out their strength with thirty or forty years' labor, they are left to shift as best they may, and are presently forgotten. No shadow of moral *right* to a support is allowed the minister of the gospel by his brethren, nor is the amount paid him regarded, either by faith or sight, as a claim that attaches, in any sense, to the yearly income of any man who professes himself to be a member of the household of faith. All that is given that way is *given*—as a charity outright.

This state of things, to say the least of it, absolutely ignores any obligation to *pay* any part of our substance to the Lord. And the Methodist Church is fast coming to the attitude of a Church which acknowledges no duty to return annually any thing for the blessing of substance and yearly increase. God charged backsliding Israel with robbery. But our Church takes higher ground, and denies *all right* upon the part of the Lord to any portion of its income.

St. Paul has placed the claim of a gospel ministry upon the same footing with that of the ministry of the Temple. They who waited at the altar had a provision made for them in the law, and yet for support were left dependent upon the voluntary obedience of the people. Tithes were not legally enforced. Gospel ministers being the ministers of Christ, are not of Levi, yet the apostle places their support upon the same basis: "Do ye not know that they which minister about holy things live of the things of the temple? EVEN SO HATH THE LORD ORDAINED that they which preach the gospel should live of the gospel." 1 Cor. ix. 13, 14. As, on the one hand, a minister of the gospel has no right to "entangle himself with the affairs of this life, that he may please Him who hath chosen him to be a soldier;" so, on the other, he has a right in gospel equity to a support out of the tribute which the people are enjoined to pay into the treasury of the Lord.

The duty of supporting those who are called by God to minister to us the precious gospel would seem to be so pleasant to a soul who feels himself under all the loving obligations of a child, that the binding letter of a law could only be superfluous. And, in truth, much is left to and expected from the love and gratitude of those who acknowledge the "perfect law of liberty." Nor would a Christian minister have it on any other wise. Olshausen beautifully remarks upon the passage, "Joanna the wife of Chuza, Herod's steward, and Susanna, and many others, which ministered to him of their substance," (Luke viii. 3 :) "He who was the spiritual life of his people disdained not to be supported by them in the body: he was not ashamed to penetrate so far into the depth of poverty as to condescend to live upon the alms of love: he only fed others in a miraculous manner; for himself, he lived upon the love of his people. Hence, he loved with a perfect and pure love, and so permitted himself to be loved: he gave all things to men, his brethren, and received all things from them, and enjoyed thereby the pure blessings of love, which is perfect then only when it is at the same time both giving and receiving. What a feature in the picture of the Messiah! Who could invent things such as these! He who feeds thousands by *one* word of his mouth, lives himself upon the bread of the poor. It was necessary to live in this manner, in order that it might be so recorded."

But the support of ministers is but one item; when a Church has done that, it has at least paid the mint and cummin—the present allowance for their support could scarcely be set down as the "weightier matters" of mercy. The Christian Church holds a vast amount of life and power and blessing in her hands, in the shape of the goods of her Lord: values upon the expenditure of which are suspended the angelic announcement of the gospel to many plains of earth where shepherds are sleeping shrouded in darkness, the reclaiming of wastes that have never bloomed as yet, and the introduction of many inquiring strangers to Him who bought them with his own blood. What has stayed her? why does she not sow gladness over the earth? Upon what passions is she expending the sums which she keeps back from her Lord? Where is the money which has been placed by him, along with the word, in her hands, with the commandment, "Go, preach the gospel to every creature?" She must pour forth both substance and soul for the world. Eternity will hold her to it. Seventy barrels of blood pass through the heart of a man in twenty-four hours; so must life be thrown out in volume, by the Church, to every extreme part of the human race. If there be any basis of duty, if any motive of love, if any strong purpose of zeal, let them be announced from the pulpit, in the class-room, and at the Conference, until the generosity " which never faileth" is acknowledged as an essential quality of Methodism.

With Mr. Goodsine, I think this is what the Methodist Church requires to make her the most efficient Church since the days of Paul. But what a vast deficiency is this! Still, vast as it is, it is within our reach. Our hope mainly is, that by preaching it to the young, liberality will characterize the next generation of Methodists. Who can predict how soon God will have mercy upon those who sit in darkness, and displace the present race of Christians with a better?

Let us come back to the least, the very least, that God claims : ONE SEVENTH OF OUR TIME AND ONE TENTH OF OUR INCOME.

Chrysostom says, on Eph. ii. 2 : "Woe to him, it is said, who doeth not alms ; and if this was the case under the Old covenant, much more is it under the New. If where the getting of wealth was allowed, and the enjoyment of it and the care of it, there was such provision made for the succoring the poor, how much more in that Dispensation where we are bidden to give up all? For what did not they of old do? They gave tithes, and tithes again upon tithes. They supported orphans, widows, and strangers; whereas some one was saying to me in astonishment, 'Why, such a one gives tithes!' What a load of disgrace does this expression imply, that a matter which with the Jews was no matter of surprise, that this should have been surprising with Christians! If there was danger then *in omitting tithes*, think how great it must be now."

Nor do I reckon as second to any the authority of the learned Grotius, one of the ablest of commentators. In his treatise on the Rights of War and Peace, chap. i., book i., he speaks of a Christian man's duty: "So likewise the old Law of the Sabbath and that of tithes are a demonstration that Christians are obliged to set apart no less than the seventh part of their time for the worship of God, nor *no less than the tenth part of their fruits or profits* for the maintenance of those who are employed in holy affairs, or for other sacred and pious uses."* Mr. Wesley, who has the authority of a Father, says, in a sermon of burning words, On the Danger of Increasing Riches: "But many have found out a way never to be rich, though their substance increase ever so much. It is this: as fast as ever money comes in, they lay it out either in land, or enlarging their business. By this means each of these, keeping himself bare of money, can still say, 'I am not rich;' yea, though he has ten, twenty, a hundred times more substance than he had some years ago. It is possible

* Lord Chief Justice Hale, Rev. Dr. Hammond, Baxter, and Doddridge, each gave one-tenth. Dr. Watts gave a fifth; Mrs. Rowe one-half.

for a man to cheat himself by this ingenious device. And he may cheat other men; for, 'as long as thou doest good unto thyself, men will speak well of thee.' But, alas! he cannot deceive the devil. Ah, no! the curse of God is upon thee already, and all that thou hast. And to-morrow, when the devil seizes thy soul, will he not say, 'What do all thy riches profit thee?' Will they purchase a pillow for thy head in the lake of fire burning with brimstone? or will they procure thee a cup of 'water to cool thy tongue while thou art tormented in that flame?' O, follow the wise direction here given, that God may not say unto thee, 'Thou fool!'

"This shift, therefore, will not avail. It will not be any protection, either against the wrath of God, or the malice and power of the devil. Thou art convicted already of 'setting thy heart' upon thy riches, if thou layest out all that thou hast above the conveniences of life, on adding money to money, house to house, or field to field, without giving *at least a tenth of thine income* (the Jewish proportion) to the poor. By whatsoever means thy riches increase—whether with or without labor, whether by trade, legacies, or any other way—unless thy charities increase in the same proportion: unless thou givest A FULL TENTH of thy substance, of thy fixed and occasional income, thou dost undoubtedly set thy heart upon thy gold, and it will 'eat thy flesh as fire!'

"But O! who can convince a rich man that he sets his heart upon riches? For considerably above half a century I have spoken on this head with all the plainness that was in my power; but with how little effect! I doubt whether I have in all that time convinced fifty misers of covetousness. When the lover of money was described ever so clearly, and painted in the strongest colors, who applied it to himself? To whom did God and all that knew him say, 'Thou art the man!'"

On this theme Mr. Wesley has written much. His sermons "On the Danger of Riches," "On Riches," on "The Use of Money," "On the Good Steward," as well as the one from which I have just quoted, indicate what his observation was of the Church in his day; and that he had a foreboding of the torpor into which the Methodists were likely to fall through covetousness. Towards the last of his ministry he gave no uncertain sound against the love of money. Not only his preaching but his example was eminently fitted to show his followers their duty. He gave away all—absolutely all. He reserved not over fifty pounds a year for his expenses, and "died not having ten pounds left." He transcended the tithe quantity by as much as the whole is greater than a tenth. Who of all his followers imitate his example? How small is the sum of them!

Has not the time come for action, if we ever hope for a reform? Let our Church recognize the principle that it is the duty of every member to pay annually one-tenth of his income as the *least* required by the gospel. How can our people be induced to make such a sacrifice? By the preachers—the example of the preachers. Let the Conferences begin it. If there were a score of preachers in each Conference pledged to each other to give to the Lord a clear tenth of their income, as in the reformation of Nehemiah—"And the Levites shall bring up the tithe of the tithes unto the house of our God," (x. 38)—the people would soon follow.*

* The effect of such an example—that of the Conference paying tithes—is not overstated. In remarking upon a certain system of systematic beneficence which

When the Methodists come to be known as a people who pay a tenth, they will be known as a Holy Ghost people. "Prove me," saith the Lord. Let us prove him. Be entreated in the words of Mr. Wesley: "Ye angels of God, ye servants of his, that continually do his pleasure: our common Lord hath intrusted you with talents far more precious than gold and silver, that you may minister in your various offices to the heirs of salvation! Do not you employ every mite of what you have received for the end for which it was given you? And hath he

---

had been recommended, the Free Church of Scotland Magazine says, "The general adoption of the principle [of systematic beneficence] would change the condition of the Church and the world. The discovery of the law of gravitation, and the application of steam to its manifold uses in modern society, have not produced a greater change on the philosophy and physical condition of mankind, than the practice of the views of pecuniary contribution here submitted to the public would effect on the *life, energy,* and *usefulness* of the Church of Christ."

not directed us to do his will on earth as it is done by you in heaven? Brethren, what are we doing? Let us awake! Let us arise! Let us imitate those flaming ministers! Let us employ our whole soul, body, and substance according to the will of our Lord! Let us render unto God the things that are God's: even all we are and all we have!"

The annual payment of one-tenth is demanded because it is the least payment by which a man can feel the King's right to an estate in his possessions. The law of tithes is based upon the constitution of the human heart, as the law of the Sabbath is upon the constitution of the human body. To pay less than one-tenth may express a measure of gratitude, while it might not be sufficient in acknowledgment of a right—the right of our Sovereign to the whole of all we have. Not to feel daily this great truth is to expose ourselves to the pride which the possession of property superinduces: it makes us forget the Almighty, and say, "What profit should we have if we pray unto him?" It will lead us to make "gold our hope, and to say to the fine gold, Thou art my confidence." How else could it be when we see in our property only a form of power, or of independence, or only the gratification of our appetites? Unless we *see* God's claim in every piece of gold, or land, or goods, we soon lose sight of God in the engrossing pursuit of wealth. When an appreciable amount of every value is felt to be God's, then he will be present to us in the work-shop, in the counting-room, in the field, and in every enterprise of commerce. The employment of the day will not shut him out. Then our duty to the Giver of all good will be seen upon the face of every piece of money as plainly as its graven "image and superscription."

It will be felt that His is the share that insures the blessing; and nine parts with a blessing are rather to be chosen than ten without. The sight of His share will keep his laws in mind amid the competition and temptation of trade: his justice will seem to sit upon it, and to assert the worth of virtuous integrity. Even losses will seem to be by his permission, and profits to flow in by his approval; thus the equally precious good of cheerful resignation or of humble gratitude will be a constant gain from the fluctuations of trade. "The blessing of the Lord it maketh rich, and he addeth no sorrow with it." Prov. x. 22.

A man may give away much during the year without acknowledging God's annual claim, and without paying it. Gifts to old servants or to poor relatives are on this wise. A man's duty to take care of those who are bound to him by natural ties, or who are in the relation of dependents, is one thing: his duty to God, to the stranger, to the world, another. The principle of giving to such as cannot make any return to us is laid down by Christ as the true one: "When ye make a feast," etc., Luke xiv. 13. The tithes of the law were a clean tenth paid into the sanctuary. To meet God's annual claim upon our income is to pay it to something that clearly represents him—the poor, the stranger, the Church, the heathen. It is hardly just to charge his account with what we furnish our own servants. We owe them a debt to support them, as well when they are helpless as when profitable. And as relationship by blood gives us a claim in the hour of need, so that claim must be met by us in the day of prosperity.

The tithe of men who are out of debt is a plain calculation; of those in debt it is one-tenth of what they actually spend for a living, for they can deny themselves a tenth, and live on less. A doctor will urge the number of poor patients which he has visited, and charge to the Lord's account the value of the practice that does not pay; which is like counting the seed that does *not* come up, for the tithe of the harvest. It is the genius of American tradesmen, planters, and men in all other pursuits, to be in debt. If debt be a bar to God's claim, it is, in this trading land, a universal one. The offerings of men may vary with their fortunes; but assuredly if they cannot bring a bullock, or lamb, they must bring a turtle-dove.

I have put down all that occurs to me on this subject.

In a subsequent letter from friend P., he says, "The wishes you have often expressed are about to be realized. Our dear Sammy has declared to his mother and myself that he feels constrained to engage in the work of the ministry. He intends shortly to offer himself to the Bishop, for China. Ever since his return from college he has been reading theological books. His evident prayerfulness, fondness for the society of the preachers, and his affectionate sadness when with his mother and myself, led me to suppose that something of the kind was working in his heart; yet, to tell the truth, I was afraid to ask him, for you know Sammy is our only son. I trusted that maybe his mother would not discover it. A few Sabbath evenings since, he told us his purpose, with tears. His mother, to my surprise, said, 'My dear boy, I gave you to the Lord when I gave you birth; I have always prayed him to make you a minister; and now I know that you are truly called to be a missionary.'

"It reminded me of the vows I made when I first felt my personal obligations to my Saviour; when I promised him the best gift at any time in my hand. Surely it is my son."

CHAPTER XII.

TAKING STOCK IN THE GOSPEL.

THE year passed on. Besides the Quarterly Conference, another important event for the temporal welfare of the circuit came with its progress. At a camp-meeting in the adjoining circuit, the preacher in charge of that circuit, Rev. Jabez Carson, became acquainted with Miss Caroline, the second daughter of Brother Badger. The young people were mutually pleased, and soon came to a definite understanding. The course of their loves ran smoothly. The old gentleman had conceived quite an admiration for the young minister, who had good natural parts. Having been prepossessed in his favor by his Christian name, and also having a great respect for the calling, Brother B. was rather proud of the proposed connection. Just before the last Quarterly Conference the event came off. They were married by the Post-Oak preacher. All the Methodists about Oakville were present; some from a distance, Hunnicut amongst the rest. All the plenty and comfort which characterizes the Englishman at home, shone conspicuously on the marriage occasion. The very idea of finding such quarters might be held as no ordinary temptation to a poor itinerant to set up his final rest. The pair were a handsome, hearty couple. The old gentleman was in his very best humor; the old lady sat up, looking as composed as she possibly could, during so momentous a passage in the experience of a housewife. After supper all began to feel easy.

"Well, squire," said the Englishman, "I am very heartily glad to see you and Sister

Wallet looking so well. I hear that you are making a fine crop too."

"O," responded the squire, "Brother Badger, there is nothing certain. I had as good a prospect in '48."

"Yes, yes," rejoined the Englishman, quickly, rather fearing some graveyard turn; "and I hear that you are out as the candidate for the Legislature: *that's* not uncertain, I hope, squire. No, no; I am very sure of that," he added, in a complimentary way, and laughing.

"O, squire," said Hunnicut, "there was a man talking to me about you the other day."

"Indeed!" exclaimed the squire; "who might that be?"

"One of your opponents."

"Ah; what did he say?" asked the squire.

"Well," said Hunnicut, "he said he was present, and heard your speech at the church, when we were raising the circuit expenses: he said it was a very fine speech, and that he was very much taken with your classical allusions."

"Was he?"

"He really was. He wanted me to tell him how much everybody subscribed, which I declined doing. He said that he heard your subscription was not large. I told him that if that was the case, he must give you credit for a good deal of independence, knowing, as you then did, that you were going to be a candidate."

"Exactly so, Mr. Hunnicut," replied the squire; "you were quite right. You see, Mr. Hunnicut," he added in a confidential tone, while Brother B. passed on, "I have had some very heavy drains on me of late years. There's disease and death, of which you have heard me speak—very well: then there is Bill and Martha, both off at school and college. Mr. Hunnicut, did you ever have to pay for schooling a child away from home?"

"My eldest is only four."

"Well, then, you don't know. Just let me tell you: how much do you suppose I mailed to-day for Bill and his sister? Five hundred dollars, I give you my word."

"Bill is a smart chap," said Hunnicut; "I know that."

"That's true, too—true enough: Bill *is* smart. But he has cost me a heap of money this last four years. Mr. Hunnicut, when he was at that military school, the amount that boy spent in buttons, yes, buttons, would have supported a smart family. You see, they used to wear a very expensive gold-washed button, with the owner's initials on the face; and, on parade, every button must shine—had to: a very particular discipline, which I always like. But the buttons often turned out to be pinchbeck—the rascals! I never saw any jewelry, Mr. Hunnicut, that was not a regular take-in: did it not get its name from the *Jews?* Well, off they had to come. Bill was vexed enough about it, but there was no help. Well, sir, the dozens of buttons I have bought, at fifteen and twenty dollars a dozen—or, rather, Bill bought, which is all the same—while at that school, no sensible man could believe. And other expenses—society fees: why, sir, the fees Bill paid would start a society from the beginning, and keep it a-going, too. One good thing, he learned all they could teach him there. So, at his request, backed by the request of the President, I took and put him to medicine. Have you ever noticed, Mr. Hunnicut, that every thing that has any leaning toward the grave is expensive? There 's military schools, medical lectures, the army, the navy, and preaching—all cost a great deal."

"Preaching, you know," said Hunnicut, "is more for life than death."

"Yes, of course," said the squire; "but somehow it always points us to the grave.

Bill has this notion: he is a very observing chap. He tells me if I would stop spending so much on preaching and such like, I should not be so cramped from his small expenses. He says it's giving him a set against all churches. Bill is quite seriously inclined, too. He wrote me a letter the other day beginning with,

> The tapering pyramid, the Egyptian's pride,
> And wonder of the world,
> Whose spiky top has wounded
> The thick cloud, and long outlived
> The angry shaking of the winter's storm,
> At last, o'erspent with the injuries
> Of time, gives way,' etc.

The opening of Blair's Grave, you remember."

"It opens finely. I should like to look into it."

"Probably you would like to look into my library. I have a fine collection on those subjects: the cholera, the yellow fever, the London plague, Herodotus on the Great

Plague, The Black Hole of Calcutta, Small-pox in the East, the African Fever, Mortuary Statistics of Pekin, Tombs, Graves, Death, Eternity, etc. You would be greatly interested, Mr. Hunnicut."

"I wonder that you find time to read so much," said H.

"The truth is, Mr. Hunnicut, I live in the past. Since the losses of '48, my thoughts constantly run back to the eventful past."

"You do not wholly neglect the present?" asked Hunnicut, with a twinkle of his eye.

"No, sir, not wholly: I use the present; but the melancholy certainty of the past, and the immense uncertainty of the future, must continually press upon every man who works a large force."

"Bill seems to view things a good deal in the same light. I am surprised that he should indulge in gloomy forebodings."

"Well, Mr. Hunnicut, Bill is a good deal pensive for such a sprightly boy: he writes that he has learned the whole of Blair's Grave by heart, and is now committing to memory Gray's Elegy on a Country Churchyard."

The Englishman here joined the group. "Well," said he, "ye were on our collection-meeting at the church. I was going to remark that the elder's speech that day was a very strong one; indeed it was! Should not a man that teaches ye, said he, have a living as much as your clerk or overseer? Indeed, it was strong. I felt it. And why not? should not a young man have a living, or a married man, when he is doing his best to preach to us? Has not he as much right to it as any of us? has not my son there, Mr. Carson, as much right to live as I, his father-in-law, or Mrs. Badger, or any of us? No, no: 'ye must not muzzle the ox,' do ye see! 'that treadeth out the corn.' 'Have we not power to eat and to drink?' says the apostle; 'have we not power to lead about a wife?' do ye see! and have her supported, too. 'Who goeth a warfare any time at his own charges?' do ye see! 'If we,' says the great Paul, 'have sown unto you spiritual things, is it a great thing if we shall reap your carnal things?' No, no; the elder was right; every word was gospel. It was a very strong speech."

The words of the Englishman caught Sister Hardiman's ear. "Now, Brother Badger," said she, "you are talking right: only talk that way, and our people will, maybe, yet come round right. They have done wonders already since this time last year."

CHAPTER XIII.

"THERE'S A BETTER DAY A-COMING."—*Chorus.*

A NEW day had dawned upon Post-Oak Circuit. In the winding up of the year the quarterage notes were mostly paid. The stewards had to advance for some, which were afterwards collected. The preacher in charge and the presiding elder were paid in full. It very soon came to be public opinion, as the elder had predicted, that a man must have a good reason for not paying his apportionment, or lose caste as a Methodist.

Those who know Post-Oak now, can hardly credit the fact that for many long years it rested under such financial gloom.

The elder remarked that "our people, at this late day, actually need to be *educated* in their duty—that many men, could they *once be started* in the right way, would improve and enlarge in their charities." This was verified in the subsequent history of Post-Oak. Four years ago, its reputation at Conference for paying the preacher was first-rate. It soon began to be noted for the size of its missionary collection. Two years since, its Conference collection was at the head of the list. This year, the preacher who was read out to "Post-Oak Circuit" was reckoned amongst the fortunate men of the Conference.

It should not be left out of this record that the spiritual prospects of the circuit began to mend about the same time with its financial. The children of many members had nearly grown up without professing religion, or even joining the Church. There was therefore a most delightful harvest reaped in the revival which began at the fourth quarterly meeting. The succeeding year they had still a better. In two years after the events herein recorded, the membership of the circuit was doubled. Very soon the meeting-houses were not large enough at the principal appointments to accommodate the congregations, and the houses were either enlarged, or wholly displaced by new, more suitable, and elegant structures.

A close observer might, with other changes, notice that there had been some alteration in the complexion of the Quarterly Conference: though all the brethren who composed *that* memorable first Quarterly Conference are still living.

On the edge of Oakville there stands a white frame-house, beautifully located in a piece of ground which measures about four acres. Several willow-oaks stand on the front line of the lot, and are reaching out their young branches toward each other. The fence, the stable, and all the out-houses are in keeping with the house, which is a tasteful specimen of rural architecture. A woodbine has been trained, and is growing luxuriantly all over the end of the porch, which extends along the whole front of the building. A lady is just now walking in the porch, and pointing a little boy of three summers to a horseman who is coming at a smart pace down a hill in the distance. It is the Rev. Jabez Carson, preacher in charge, who is returning from a round on the circuit to the Post-Oak Parsonage.

The final departure of the Rev. Zelophehad Crane was an event in the history of the Oakville appointment only second in its importance to that of his first arrival. It appeared to the satisfaction of the First Church that the ex-"highly popular pastor" of Lynn had, in all, six entire, three half, and three one-quarter sermons. These, with his "serials," constituted his complete stock of wares. After their first blinding effect, it was discovered by the session that they were themselves moving on in a circle—the emblem of eternity—the last of one series being but the precursor of the first of the other. The parson was waited on at the conclusion of the seventh round. He offered to furnish any amount of new material, if the session would furnish him with new *subjects*: that his present courses of sermons and lectures had been selected and arranged exhaustively, with an especial view to exhaust the entire circle of history, science, ethics, and theology This proposition was triumphantly unanswerable. About the twelfth round a call providentially arose from a town where the "learned pastor" had lectured once. After great hesitation, correspondence, wish for Divine guidance, reluctant consent, etc., etc., the call, being slightly increased, was accepted. To follow the fortunes of the reverend gentleman: in the course of the year after, he received another call, which he accepted, still following the star of duty. This proved a very effectual call, as it was the last ever made the "beloved pastor." He found in the congregation an old planter who had fifty negroes, and a daughter, of otherwise ordinary attractions, his only child. The parson courted and married her. The old planter died. Then from all the North-east the Cranes came, one by one, like the first birds of the season. One is a schoolmaster, another the settled pastor of the church, a third has married a cousin of Mrs. Zelophehad, another is trying to marry another cousin, and another is an agent for a corn-crusher, with the right of the State. They are all pretty much "in the one calling." The old man himself presently came down to Egypt. They say he likes it. Soon after his arrival, he remarked that "Colored help can't do as much work in a day as white help, by more than half." It is thought by some that at present the Crane family are doing but little to dispel the moral darkness of the great South-west.

The pastor who now fills the pulpit of the First Church of Oakville, immediately succeeded the one whose history wound up so prosaically. He was on a visit to Oakville, when, during his preaching, a sinner was cut to the heart by the word, and presently professed "peace." Being a true minister of the cross, as well as a theological graduate, he reckoned the incident an indication that God called him to that field. Upon the application of the session, he accepted their call. Happy day was it for the religious interests of the whole region, when he became the pastor of the First Church at Oakville. He provokes the Methodist preacher to love and good works. A good preacher, a constant pastor, a studious, im proving, holy man, our preachers have to work hard to preach acceptably with him in the same town and the same day. Not long since, he improved a Sabbath when our people would be at liberty to attend the First Church, to preach upon the "just measure of Christian benevolence." He gave our people a high fall. In the course of his sermon, he illustrated by citing Mr. Wesley: his devotion to doing good; the large sums which he gave away; and lauded him until the Methodists were in raptures. "And yet," said he, "I show unto you a more excellent way. Behold one who gave away five times as much as John Wesley—Mr. Amos Lawrence, of Boston."

He then read from President Hopkins's discourse upon the life of this remarkable man. Text: "When the ear heard me, it blessed me; and when the eye saw me, it gave witness to me; because I delivered the poor that cried, and the fatherless, and him that had none to help him. The blessing of him that was ready to perish came upon me, and I caused the widow's heart to sing for joy." Job xxix. 11–13.

"The features in the life of Mr. Lawrence which, notwithstanding his desire and endeavors to avoid notoriety, distinguished him above all other men of his time, were the extent, the variety, and the manner of his munificence. In these respects we have not known his equal.

"Having acquired an ample fortune—as much as he supposed would 'be good for his descendants'—he determined, many years before his death, not to allow his property to increase by accumulation, but to expend the whole of his income in donations for the benefit of others. To aid him in carrying out this resolution to the letter, and in accordance with the system which marked all his business transactions, he was accustomed to take an accurate account of his property at the beginning of each year. The follow ing is his entry, January 1, 1852:

"'The value of my property is somewha! more than it was a year ago, and I pray God that I may be faithful in its use. My life seems now more likely to be spared for a longer season than for many years past and I never enjoyed myself more highly Praise the Lord, O my soul!

"'P. S. The outgoes for all objects, since January 1, 1842—ten years—have been six hundred and four thousand dollars, more than five-sixths of which have been applied to making other people happy; and it is no trouble to find objects for all I have to spare.'

"He survived one year longer, and died before the dawn of the next New Year's day. From a comparison of the above statement with the details on which it was founded, and with subsequent entries, it is ascertained that the amount of his expenditures for charitable purposes, during the last eleven years of his life, was five hundred and twenty-five thousand dollars! From 1829 to 1842, he gave one hundred and fourteen thousand dollars; and, considering his known liberality and habits of systematic charity, from the very beginning of his career, it is 'safe to assert that, during his life, he expended SEVEN HUNDRED THOUSAND DOLLARS for the benefit of his fellow-men!' "

"What do you think of that, Brother Goodsine," asked Sister Hardiman, as soon as church was out. "Is that true, that a Congregationalist has surpassed Mr. Wesley?"

"I hope so," he replied: "'would that all the Lord's people were prophets.' It is high time the Congregationalists, or some other people, were doing it; for there are no Methodists that I know of either surpassing or approaching the example of Mr. Wesley. Mr.

Amos Lawrence, I doubt not, gave away more dollars than Mr. Wesley, and may be favorably compared with him as a Christian giver. Thank God, the right stock has not yet run out! it flourishes in our day. The Congregationalists and Presbyterians are ahead of us in this matter. It is no uncommon thing to hear of their people giving tens of thousands at a time, to endow colleges, to advance missions, or to build churches. With us it is a rare thing. Can it be that the Holy Spirit has cut us out after a smaller pattern!"

"Mr. Wesley was no scant pattern."

"No, sister, no; but the race of Wesleys is nearly extinct. *We* are not Wesleys."

The graveyard at Postville has been handsomely enclosed. There is a tomb there of white marble, which rises out of a smooth green sod, surrounded by a light railing. The inscription on it is as follows:

HERE LIES
THE REV. WILLIAM HYMES,
A Member of the Red River Conference,
Our dear Minister,
Who died in Postville
Of Yellow Fever,
Aug. 25, 1847,
In the midst of his usefulness,
Aged 23 years.
This is to his Memory,
By the
MEMBERS OF THE POST-OAK CIRCUIT.

It was in the early morning when a gray-headed negro and two plough-boys alighted from their teams, and came into the grave-yard. As they approached the tomb, they laid their hats upon the ground.

"Ah, boys," exclaimed the old man, in a subdued tone, as he put his hand upon the railing, "*this* was our friend."

"What was it he told you, daddy?" asked one of them.

"'Uncle John,' said he, 'I am very glad to see you: I shall never preach to you again.' 'O, Mr. Hymes,' said I, 'I am very sorry to see you so ill: you have been a very comforting preacher to me, sir.' 'It is a great comfort to me now to hear you say that, Uncle John,' said he. All the time," added the old man, "his face was happy and his mind strong. 'Tell my brethren,' he said, 'that you saw me die on the circuit. O yes, I could die twice to save one sinner!'"

While the old man spoke, the tears fell like rain. Presently he dropped on his knees in silent prayer, and the boys followed. In a few moments they were on their teams, singing, as the sun rose upon the field:

"He's gone, he's gone, his work is done;
He's fought his fight, his race is run;
And out of sight, beyond the sun,
He's living now, in glory!

CHAPTER XIV.

TOO MANY EFFECTUAL DOORS OPEN—MISSIONARY MALT A DESIDERATUM—RUNNING TWO SAWS.

To no one was the circuit more attached or more indebted than to Brother Jacob Oakhart, "the negro preacher."

Very little has been said in this history of him, excepting to give his own account of his own sermon. Whenever he preached or exhorted—for he was only an exhorter—a large number of white persons were present; and it gave him an opportunity, which he improved, of hitting the white brethren while preaching to the colored. His missionary sermons, which came off once a year, usually drew nearly the whole of the white congregation, as they were announced the week before; and Brother Oakhart usually "spread himself" on the occasion. Though the white brethren of course felt that nothing that was said was meant for them, yet it was evident that the rough eloquence of the "negro preacher" told favorably upon the masters and mistresses—fully as much as the tamer and smoother speech of their own pulpit. It was on such a missionary occasion at the beginning of the year, after the quarterly meeting, etc., that Brother Oakhart preached from 1 Cor. xvi. 9: "For a great door and effectual is opened unto me, and there are many adversaries."

"Take the map of the world, my brethren, the geography hung on the wall, and, if it's not too old, measure the fly-specs on it, and you have the bigness of the mission-stations of the Church. We have been shut out a great deal from different countries, for which we ought to be thankful; for if we had not been shut out, it would have been all the same thing—we never should have gone in. But now, hear it in grief, the doors are open, and a good many of them at that. First, there is China : the Chinese, olive-skins, and their eyes set cornering. There's where we get our tall fowls from. They can nearly all read—better schools than we have in this country even—people thick as bees, and as industrious—babies in the way—they stuff rice in their babies' mouths, and choke them to death on purpose. Very smart people, but they kill their children ; bury their dead kin near the house, and keep them like sweet-potatoes ; write their names on a board, their grandfathers' names, and pray to the board. They need this gospel. Next, there's Siam : Siamese twins, you know. The King of Siam says, Come along. Then we have Birmah : Brahma—Brahma-Pootra—only they never eat chickens, lest they should eat some friend whom they believe has been turned into one.

Then India; where mace and cocoanuts and nutmegs grow, and the air is spiced; there are countless thousands crawling in the dust before grim idols and cruel wheels. Then Madagascar, where the queen could eat a missionary, but the young king has joined the Church. Then Africa, where you all came from; there the people are thick as leaves on the trees, and are counted only as the sands of Sahara; there they sell each other, and eat each other on a pinch; there when a king dies they kill two or three dozen of his servants to go along and wait on him. There you have boa-constrictors, and lions, and orang-outangs, and elephants, and every sort of terrible things—but no missionaries, except a few crouched up in one corner. Then South America, where the pope and the devil reign turn about; some chance there—not much; a good deal in Mexico, New Granada, and Nicaragua. So long as the Church won't do any thing there, I am glad there's a chance of United States soldiers doing something. Then the Sandwich Islands; some chance of their being annexed; there they have a pure gospel. Then Borneo, where every respectable citizen has a string of skulls and gourds hanging up in the porch to dry. Plants half the year, and pirates half; lays by his crop, rows off in his war-canoe, he and his neighbors; lands on some island, burns their houses, robs and murders till he is satisfied, comes home, gathers in his crop, and triumphantly dries his skulls. The English have sent a frigate, and, while the Church has been holding missionary meetings, have cannonaded the haunts of these bloodthirsty wretches and opened the doors to the Church. The Lord makes the wrath of man to praise him.

"Thus, by one thing and another, cannons and Bibles, merchants and missionaries, treaties and traffic, guns and guano, men-of-war and men of God, the world has been opened, its doors have been unlocked or forced until they stand wide, thousands of them, open wide to the Church. What is wanted? Money. What will send the light of heaven into bloody Borneo? Money. What will keep rice out of the babies' mouths? Money. What will send the pope and the devil to the same bed? Money. Money will print Bibles in every tongue, and send them to every land. Money will raise the standard of a crucified Saviour—Him that was sold for money shall by money be lifted to the gaze of dying myriads. Sinful silver owes us that.

"But where is the money? In every house, in every pocket. There's many a wedge of gold hid. There is scarcely a Church society, even the smallest, but you may see in it a Dives. Jerusalem had one. This Christian land can send ten thousand to keep him of Jerusalem company, and have enough left to make a full crop the next year. Whence came all this money? What! so pious, and so rich too! If you are pious, how came you rich? If you are rich, how keep you pious? How keep you your piety and your riches together? Hark! 'You have robbed me!' Who art thou, Lord? 'I am Jesus, whom thou hast robbed.' Wherein have we robbed thee? 'Behold, the hire of the laborers who have reaped down your fields, which is of you kept back by fraud, crieth; and the cries of them which have reaped are entered into the ears of the Lord of Sabaoth. Ye have heaped treasure together for the last days. Ye have lived in pleasure on the earth, and been wanton. Your gold and silver is cankered; and the rust of them shall be a witness against you, and shall eat your flesh as it were fire. You eat up my people as you eat bread. Ye are cursed with a curse; for ye have robbed me, even this whole nation.' The Church robs God of the money that was put into her hands for the benefit of the world. She has become a den of robbers. 'What, the Christian Church?' *Christian* indeed! If the whole Christian Church of this country goes on at the rate she has been, giving three millions of dollars a year for the conversion of the world, it will take a thousand years for her to give as much as the Jewish Church gave to build the Temple of Jerusalem! Do you call that Christian? three thousand millions for the Temple: three millions for a dying universe!

"I am glad, brethren, that you are black, and not white, that you are poor and not rich, that you are the servants and not the rulers, that you are owned and not owners. You will have enough to answer for, without answering for the blood and bones of the heathen, their miseries and murders, their dreadful darkness, old ulcers, devil-worship, and grub-worm soup.

"Under ground they read the missionary reports! the tears in the report of the secretary, and the coppers in the report of the treasurer! They do not read "Punch," but "Reports." They know down there how much everybody has, and they watch how much everybody gives.

"The Church is agoing to do something, for she is an angel having the everlasting gospel. She is clad in orient robes, has a sweet face, washes in clouds of rosy dew, sings the divine airs of another world, and speaks eloquently of the kingdoms of this world, soon to become the kingdoms of our God and of his Christ. She intends a large flight presently, to unfold her message. She sings and plumes herself, and plumes herself and sings. O, what a blessing she has in store for every heathen wretch! Yet never flies. For her anklets and bracelets are of heavy gold, and a thousand ingots are sewed up in her girdle. John's angel swept the mid-heavens; but this beautiful creature trails along the ground. To the poor heathen the gates of heaven swing heavily on their *golden* hinges.

"O ye children of the sun, who have drunk in the light until your skins are black, so is it with the hearts of the race called Christians. The love of self drinks in all. The love of money breeds more darkness than one world can hold. What! will they make a mint of heaven, and coin the pavement of the City of the great King? Ay, they will! they do! By every unpitied barbarian that dies the Church saves money. O, if there were no foreign sinners! then would the Church's crown appear in greater lustre! The conversion of the heathen will be, perhaps, the most costly piece of work on the earth when completed. Missionaries it might cost, (for them we could afford,) did it not cost so much money. 'O dreadful cry for money! My good Christian money! O my money! must I send thee out on a mission to fools—maybe on a fool's mission!

O heaven-born Charity, pity us! Help the heathen, for mercy's sake! Help all of us, O do! This Pagan load never fell upon our Church till now; I never felt it till now. Would the heathen were well saved and hearsed! If they are to be saved on this wise, we are ruined! if they are ruined, we shall not be saved; so, any way, we are ruined. Who are these heathen, anyhow? Who says heathen? Was I not a heathen? Did I not take my chance? Who helped *me?* Were we not all heathens once? Who helped us? They have their chance. Am I now to be taxed, made poor—in fact, turned into a heathen again?—for what? For the heathen! Turn a good Christian into a heathen, to turn a heathen into a Christian! No, *sir:* I am a heathen myself. I will be the heathen. I want more preaching myself: send *me* the gospel; call me heathen; don't be afraid—I'll stand it. It costs nothing to be a heathen; but, O misery, to be a Christian! It used to cost nothing to be a Christian. But these last days—since missions, and Bible societies, and tracts, and travelling agents, and secretaries, to every form of heathen, have gathered the Church—I am ruined!* absolutely stripped! I have given away all I am worth; we are starved; we make nothing; I have not made a cent in two years. Who will bury us: the heathen? Who will feed us: the heathen? Who will send us the gospel when we run out: the heathen? Not a bit of it. No, *sir:* get me

* Being "ruined" by over-giving: not an unusual fear, though in most cases a little premature. The following should sink into such as either have been ruined, or fear they will be, by too much liberality:

"Brethren, [said the speaker,] I have heard of churches starving out from a saving spirit; but I have never heard of one dying of benevolence. And if I could hear of one such, I would make a pilgrimage to it by night, and in that quiet solitude, with the moon shining and the aged elm waving, I would put my hands on the moss-clad ruins, and, gazing on the venerable scene, would say, 'Blessed are the dead who die in the Lord!'"

to heaven if you can, but don't rob me on the way.'

"Thus,

"'O'er dreary wastes they weep each other's woe.'*

"'They lusted exceedingly in the wilderness, and tempted God in the desert. He gave them their request; but sent leanness into their souls.' Psalm cvi. 14, 15. The angel has rolled back the stone from the door, but the Church prefers to stay a while in her sepulchre.

"For every apostle there are a legion of 'adversaries.' Who enters this door enters it in the face of a scowling crowd. Difficulties there may be, covetous croakers there are; but let him who loves Christ enter boldly. Enter, that no man may take thy crown. Send out life, that you may shine as the firmament. Deny thyself, that multitudes may rise up in the judgment and call

* Pope.

thee blessed. Better in that day be blessed, than cursed of the heathen. Part with earth; suffer the pang; and take the heavenly pathway of duty.

"And now for the collection. Aunt Minty's master was once taking up a missionary hat-collection among our white brethren; as he passed her by, the old lady called to him, and put in the hat six fresh eggs. The old lady was not behind the times. In England they use eggs to get up a missionary feeling. Missionary breakfast at the London Hotel: every thing on the table made out of eggs. Ham and eggs, turkey, duck, chicken, pheasant, turtle-soup, chicken-salad, sponge-cake, frozen custard, egg-nog, etc. With wisdom, wit, wine, and victuals, their bowels move toward a world in want. You cannot move the hearts of some people until you stir their stomachs. The Lord was merciful in this matter. Had great barbacues at the Temple. Priests read the law; the people listened: they knew that the dinner was getting done. Maybe we in this country work too much on a cold collar and an empty stomach. Who knows but Jonathan has a genius for giving after dinner? Most of our missionary addresses sound like after-dinner speeches; only we have no religious wines in this country, and all our liquors are sinful. No Barclay, Perkins & Co.'s Entire. Poor heathen! O, if we had some good religious malt liquor to help out our missionary spirits! Missionary meetings in this country, monstrous dry work. The Goths drank their savage wines out of the skulls of their enemies. Enough Indian skulls about Oakville to give a tun of sweet-potato beer a fine missionary flavor. This zeal is too dry; too dry, depend upon it; must line it with something pleasant. The Evil Spirit is seeking dry places. English people give him no quarter. Smoking meats and large sacrifices—'to your health and the heathen.

Duty made easy; salvation of the world made pleasant.

"We can try next time. What you do now must be done dry; just so. Nothing but the plaintive wants of the unhappy: only to ring over their dark wastes, 'To you this day is born a Saviour, which is Christ the Lord.' Dry work, brethren; but I reckon you'll do it. As your Saviour asks you, please to tell the poor souls of his death and love."

Among the hearers of Brother Oakhart was Colonel Hector G. W. Barb. The Colonel had honored the occasion with his presence. The Colonel gave something at the proper time. The boy who carried the hat around, looked up at the slight sound, and saw the Colonel's face. The Colonel had a face. The Colonel was rich as cream; lived pretty much on cream; and ate his own cream. The Colonel was moral; could talk you an hour on pure religion; he liked to see that kind. The Colonel did not like so much trapping in some churches—pews, and your high-salaried clergy; costly edifices, frescoed, with choirs, and damask—all wrong. "The house of God, sir, should be substantial; plain, neat, and cheap, like our own houses."

The Colonel was so kind as to express himself pleased with the sermon. "Strong, practical, pointed discourse; nourishing, rough, and plain as the food we eat." Had never heard the "negro preacher" before, but had heard of him.

The Colonel was not a member of any Church. Mrs. Hector G. W. Barb was—of the First Church of Oakville. The Colonel, however, was, on a Sabbath morning, a regular attendant at the Methodist. "Its primitive, apostolical, popular, experimental, and zealous ministry, doctrines, and discipline, are the very thing, sir, for plain and unpretending men like myself."

The Colonel's house was an imposing structure of brick, stuccoed and washed white, with a row of pillars supporting airy porches on three sides. It was furnished with every costly comfortable thing, and suggested wealth and ease whichever way the eye turned. The parlor windows opened on lawns, shaded with grand old pecan-trees, and gardens which showed that no culture or pains were spared to secure whatever was rare or beautiful. The Colonel usually rode the best horse and drove the finest carriage in the settlement. When one of the bishops once passed through that part of the country, the Colonel had him to dinner. The Colonel talked in great admiration of Methodism, its missions to the slave, its itinerancy, and its pioneering spirit:—the Bishop wished so much that the Colonel were a member, and thought what a tower of strength the Colonel would be to the cause in those parts. The new preacher, whoever he might be, or the new elder, when he saw on what a horse the Colonel rode to church, and in what a house the Colonel lived, and what a fine, tall, well-favored, dignified-looking gentleman the Colonel was, usually preached right at the Colonel for the first three months. The Colonel would let you preach to his negroes on the plantation, or let them go to the meeting-house, one or the other, as you pleased. The preachers tried preaching in the Colonel's sugar-house for two years.

The ruling elder of the First Church took occasion to ask the Colonel for Mrs. Barb's contribution for the support of their pastor. He had been referred to the Colonel by the Colonel's lady: she never gave any thing herself, but left it to the Colonel, in such matters, to do what he thought right. "We are greatly in arrears to our pastor, I assure you, Colonel."

"You know, sir, that *my* preferences are all Methodistic. Mrs. Barb, to be sure, does not agree with me; she attends your Church, and I do not object: in matters of religion we should all be spontaneous and unconstrained."

"I was not questioning your preferences, Colonel; it was only on account of your lady that we expected you to aid us."

"Well, I am unfortunate, I confess," rejoined the Colonel. "The First Church comes, on one side, on account of Mrs. Barb, and one of the Methodist stewards on the other side, on my own account: really, you gentlemen of the Church are rather hard; you are running two saws on me. However, I suppose I must do something. I will speak with Mrs. Barb about it."

"Have you any thought of trying Colonel Hector G. W. to-day?" asked John Bear of Brother Goodsine, as they came out of the church.

"Yes, possibly," answered the old man. "I suppose patience should have its perfect work in that case. The Colonel has never yet paid the missionary any thing for preaching to his negroes."

"So great an admirer, too, of missions to the slave," said John Bear. "I see the ruling elder has just had a pull at him; but the Colonel is such a strong Methodist in his feelings, I rather think the elder didn't bag much game."

In riding home it so happened that Brother Goodsine fell in with the Colonel. The old man had long since dispensed with all ceremony in this case. After some weather preliminaries, and much high compliment upon the "negro preacher" by the Colonel, "Well, Colonel Barb," said the old man, "we are still expecting something from you on the old missionary account, and for our last year's preacher."

"Our duty, sir, to support the gospel; though I fear, Mr. Goodsine, that your preachers are getting out of the good old ways: it's taking more money to support them than it used to in the days of Asbury."

"If it does, I do not know where they get it," replied the old man: "where do you suppose it comes from, Colonel?"

"I'm sure, sir, I know not; I only surmised and feared that such was the case. I wish to see Methodist preachers poor and plain and pious, such as they used to be in Georgia in the days of old Hope Hull."

"Any amount you may pay, Colonel, I can promise, shall go to settle a bill for the mere necessaries of life."

"O, as to that, it is a small matter—we are peculiar and unfortunate: Mrs. Barb has become a member of the First Church, and I, you know, am of *you*. Here are two sets and sorts of claims and applications—very much like running two saws on us, Mr. Goodsine. However, Mrs. Barb and I must talk the matter over."

"I will tell you, Colonel Barb," replied the

old man, smiling good-humoredly, "I think it is *you* that are running the saws, not we."

After they parted company, the old man rode on alone, shaking his sides. "Well, well, did ever any one hear the like of that! Colonel Hector George Washington Barb actually running two saws! Well, well."

CHAPTER XV.

THE SETTING SUN.

An old man leaning on his staff sat at the door of a small cottage in Oakville.

> "Great grace that old man to him given had;
> For God he often saw from heaven's hight;
> All were his earthly eien both blunt and bad,
> And through great age had lost their kindly sight."

It was old Father Hemphill. His grand-daughter Molly, a sweet girl of eleven, had just finished giving him his bread and milk supper.

"Has the sun gone down yet, my darling?"

"No, Grandpa," replied Molly, "he is just beginning to touch the hills with his lower edge."

"I thought so; is not the sky very clear?"

"Yes, Grandpa, there is not a cloud to be seen."

"Then I can see a little, my darling. O, how sublime is the great arch of the sky! Nothing in nature so enlarges our sense of being; it seems to give us room; the height of it is so satisfying to the desire which man has for an unbounded home. In thinking over all the objects which I most miss from dimness of sight, next to your sweet face and your mother's, my darling, I oftenest wish to see once more the blue sky. What a delightful balmy day this has been, darling! I love the fall of the year in this Southern latitude, more than any other season. In the North they have but an imperfect notion of this delightful temperature; the sensation is to me that of bathing in air."

"Did you ever live in the North, Grandpa?" asked Molly.

"O yes, my darling; there are few sections

of country, in the North or South, in the East or West, where grandpa has not been at some time. For forty-five years I received an appointment as an itinerant preacher from our dear bishops. But from the waters of the Monongahela down to the Attakapas country the greater part of my life as a preacher was spent."

"I think you said the Attakapas was a tribe of Indians, Grandpa: did you use to preach to the Indians?"

"Yes, indeed, Grandpa has many a time preached through an interpreter. Many a time have I slept in the woods; for years, as often there as elsewhere. This whole country was then thinly settled. I labored hereabouts, and all over the West and South-west, among the early settlers."

"Was it not a hard life, Grandpa?" asked Molly.

"It was a very glorious life, my dearest; yes, a hard life, but a useful, noble toil. O, would that I could still preach the gospel to poor sinners, and minister consolation to the people of God!"

"Were you poor then too, Grandpa?"

"Yes, my dear, I was poor then too—often very poor; though sometimes I had a little beforehand. I have been once or twice, of late, rather more dependent than any time before. For when I was younger and could go from place to place, God always opened the heart of some Lydia, or some Widow of Sarepta, to shelter and feed me. But, my darling, God is still good, and the pleasures of memory, at the close of a life which has been spent in trying to do good, are calm and sweet to the soul as this fall-sunset."

"But just the thought of being poor in old age, Grandpa, makes me wish not to live to be old if I am to be poor," said Molly. "Now suppose, Grandpa, you had neither ma nor me to wait on you, and give you your bread and milk: what *could* you do?"

"Ah, my darling, the Lord has many ways. He will fulfil his promises; and he has said that he will not see the righteous forsaken."

"O, Grandpa!" exclaimed Molly, "I think I see old Mrs. Hardiman and another lady coming—the new preacher's wife, I think."

The two ladies came upon a rather unusual mission: they were bringing the old, worn-out itinerant a new suit of clothes, and, what was still better, were the bearers of a letter containing a year's quarterage, (old style,) one hundred dollars.

"I wonder if the old man is at home," said Mrs. Carson.

"O, yes," answered Sister Hardiman; "he does not often stir out. He is very systematic; and I expect, as it's sunset, we shall find the old man eating his bread and milk. Sweet old man! he never complains. O, how often have I prayed for such a day as this! and now the Lord has heard me. Our people are awakening to their duty;

and, what is better, beginning to realize the pleasure and spiritual profit which flow from doing it. But here is the cottage of his daughter."

> "There they doe find that goodly aged sire,
> With snowy lockes adowne his shoulders shed;
> As hoary frost with spangles doth attire
> The mossy brannches of an oke half-ded."

After the usual salutations, the ladies told the old man the object of their visit, and handed him the suit of clothes and the money-letter.

"Molly, my darling," said the old man, "did I not just tell you that the Lord had many ways to fulfil his promises? Molly," continued he, addressing the ladies, "gets a little frightened sometimes, when she sees the meal getting low in the barrel. But," he added, "this is no ordinary supply. It has been a long time since my dear brethren sent me so much—if, indeed, ever. Tell my dear friends of Post-Oak that, with Paul, I can say, 'I rejoice in the Lord greatly that now, at the last, your care of me hath flourished again. Not that I speak in respect of want; for I have learned in whatsoever state I am, therewith to be content. I know both how to be abased and I know how to abound: everywhere and in all things I am instructed both to be full and to be hungry, both to abound and to suffer need. I can do all things through Christ which strengtheneth me. Notwithstanding ye have well done that ye did communicate with my affliction. Not because I desire a gift; but I desire fruit that may abound to your account. But I have all and abound: I am full, having received the things which were sent from you, an odor of a sweet smell, a sacrifice acceptable, well-pleasing to God.'"

"What a fine old man!" exclaimed Mrs. Carson, as they left the house. "It is worth half a life of common pleasure to be the bearer of a gift to such a noble spirit. How much like an aged apostle he looked when he repeated that beautiful scripture, and gave us his blessing!"

She waited for an answer from Sister Hardiman, and then saw that the old lady was weeping.

PUBLICATIONS

OF THE

Methodist Episcopal Church, South.

THE HEBREW MISSIONARY: Essays, Exegetical and Practical, on the Book of Jonah. By the Rev. Joseph Cross, D.D. 18mo., pp. 242. Price 40 cts.

This book is a valuable contribution to our Church literature—it exhibits great research, and abounds in eloquent passages and valuable reflections. The engravings and maps illustrative of Nineveh, as brought to light by Layard and others, add great interest to the work.

HOME; OR THE WAY TO MAKE HOME HAPPY. By the Rev. David Hay. With an Introduction by the Rev. Alfred Barrett. Price 30 cts.

The author, as well as his endorser, is an estimable Wesleyan minister in England. His treatise ought to be in every *home* where the English language is spoken.

MEMOIRS OF THE REV. THOMAS SPENCER, of Liver pool. By Thomas Raffles, LL. D., his Successor in the Pastoral Office. Price 30 cts.

A beautiful narrative of the brief and brilliant career of a lovely young minister, who was drowned in the Mersey.

FRANK NETHERTON; or, the Talisman. Price 40 cts

The principal character of this work is beautifully drawn, and in it a boy's religion is charmingly described.

LESSONS FROM NATURE: in Six Narratives. By the Author of "The Week." Price 40 cts.

A revised edition of one of Mrs. Cheap's engaging and instructive volumes.

WONDERS OF ORGANIC LIFE. Price 35 cts.

The phenomena of organic life, in numerous particulars, are happily brought to view in this admirable volume.

THE CHRISTIAN FATHER'S PRESENT TO HIS CHILDREN. By J. A. James. Price 50 cts.

This work is written in a graceful style, and is full of excellent suggestions, cautions, and counsels. A few editorial notes and corrections have been made where the author's theological views appeared to be defective, and inconsistent with the general strain of the volume.

PLANTS AND TREES OF SCRIPTURE. Price 30 cts.

In revising this work, the editor has arranged the subjects in alphabetical order, and illustrated the letter-press by a great many elegant engravings, executed expressly for this edition.

GLIMPSES OF THE DARK AGES. Price 35 cts.

THE WORLD OF WATERS. By Fanny Osborne. With illustrations. Two vols. 18mo., pp. 186, 224. Price 70 cts.

A couple of fascinating and instructive volumes. The tales and narratives beguile, like sailors' yarns, the voyage over the world of waters. The descriptions and anecdotes blend the charm of romance with the credibility of truth. The illustrations are superb.

MEMOIR OF JOHN HUSS. Price 30 cts.

ANCIENT BRITISH CHURCH. Price 30 cts.

FAMILY GOVERNMENT. By Bishop Andrew. Price 30 cts.

BEREAVED PARENTS CONSOLED. By the Rev. John Thornton. Carefully revised: with an Introduction and Selection of Lyrics for the Bereaved. By T. O. Summers, D.D. 18mo., pp. 144. Price, full gilt, 40 cts.; in extra binding, 75 cts.; gilt backs, 30 cts.—24mo., pp. 144. Price, in muslin, 25 cts.

This is an elegant volume. Its contents are adapted to administer comfort to the Jacobs and Rachels who weep for their children because they are not. They will scarcely "refuse to be comforted" by the consolatory topics so judiciously presented in this excellent work.

THE STEAM ENGINE. Edited by Thomas O. Summers, D. D. 18mo., pp. 188. Price 30 cts.

A capital companion in a steamboat or car.

LIFE AND TIMES OF LEO THE TENTH. Price 30 cts.

A competent pen, like that which produced this volume, could scarcely fail to make an interesting book on such a theme as this.

LIFE AND TIMES OF CHARLEMAGNE. Price 30 cts.

It contains as much information concerning the great Charles and his times as one might desire.

THE CRUSADES. Price 40 cts.

A concise, judicious history of the *holy wars.*

ILLUSTRATIONS OF LYING IN ALL ITS BRANCHES. By Amelia Opie. Price 45 cts.

A cheap and handsome edition of this great classic.

SKETCHES FOR YOUTH. By Cæsar Malan. Price 25 cts.

FANNY, THE FLOWER-GIRL; and the Infant's Prayer. By Selina Bunbury. Price 20 cts.

CONVENIENT FOOD. Price 20 cts.

The foregoing are narratives for the little folks, equally useful and entertaining.

THE CLAREMONT TALES; or, Illustrations of the Beatitudes. Price 30 cts.

These populâr tales occupy a high rank in the species of religious literature to which they belong.

BOATMAN'S DAUGHTER: A Narrative for the Learned and Unlearned. By Alfred Barrett. 18mo., pp. 132. Price 30 cts.

Good judges have assigned this book a place with the "Dairyman's Daughter"—a sufficient recommendation. It is adorned with a handsome Frontispiece.

THE PILGRIM'S PROGRESS FROM THIS WORLD TO THAT WHICH IS TO COME. Delivered under the Similitude of a Dream. By John Bunyan. New edition, with a Biographical Introduction by Thomas O. Summers, D.D., and handsome illustrations. 18mo. In two Parts. Part I., pp. 272. Part II., pp. 242.

This Christian classic is presented in a very elegant dress. The two parts are bound in separate volumes, for the convenience of Sunday-school libraries. Price 30 cts. per volume. It is also bound in one volume, pp. 514. Price 60 cts.

BIBLE READINGS FOR EVERY DAY IN THE YEAR. Specially designed for Children. 6 vols., 196 pp. each. Price $2.00 for the entire set.

These readings go all through the Bible. The language is remarkable for its beautiful simplicity. The volumes are illustrated by a dozen fine engravings. The set is a capital present to a child.

THE SUNDAY-SCHOOL TEACHER; or, the Catechetical Office. By Thomas O. Summers, D.D. 18mo., pp. 144. Price 30 cts.

This work discusses the most interesting questions connected with the Catechetical System—the Teacher's Qualifications, Difficulties, and Encouragements. It exhibits the obligations of pastors and teachers to the children of the Church, and shows how they may be discharged.

HOME TRUTHS. By the Rev. J. C. Ryle, B. A. 18mo. pp. 324. Price 50 cts.

This book is full of plain, pointed observations, strikingly adapted to elicit serious thought, and to induce holy living.

LONDON IN THE OLDEN TIME; or, Sketches of the English Metropolis, from its Origin to the End of the Sixteenth Century. Price 35 cts.

LONDON IN MODERN TIMES; or, Sketches of the great Metropolis during the last two Centuries. Price 35 cts.

These are life-like "Sketches"—a couple of sterling volumes The engravings of the Crystal Palace and London Bridge are elegant

FIFTY BEAUTIFUL BALLADS. Price 40 cts.

FIFTY FINE POEMS. Price 40 cts.

A couple of elegant volumes, containing some of the cream of English poetry. They are adorned with numerous embellishments

CEREMONIES OF MODERN JUDAISM. By Herman Baer. With an Introduction by Thomas O. Summers Price 45 cts.

The author—an educated Israelite, though now a Christian—is familiarly acquainted with the ceremonies of modern Judaism: he has described them with accuracy. Some elegant engravings embellish the interesting volume.

CHARACTERS, SCENES, AND INCIDENTS OF THE REFORMATION. Two vols. Price 60 cts.

MEMOIR OF OLD HUMPHREY; with Gleanings from his Portfolio, in Prose and Verse. 18mo., pp. 272. Price 40 cents.

The perusal of this beautiful biography will give an interest to the various publications of Mr. Mogridge, not inferior to that thrown around them by the previous *incognito* of the author. The copy, of which this is a faithful reprint, is one of *the new edition* of the London Religious Tract Society, in whose service the subject of the Memoir employed, for many years, his ready and prolific pen. The Memoir should accompany our uniform edition of Old Humphrey's Works—a capital series, which should be in every Sunday-school and Family Library: they are as follows:

Cheerful Chapters, 30 cts.; Country Tales for the Young, 30 cts.; Chapters for Children, 30 cts.; Old Michael and Young Maurice, 35 cts.; Thoughts for the Thoughtful, 40 cts.; Old Humphrey's Observations, 40 cts.; Old Humphrey's Addresses, 40 cts.; Old Humphrey's Walks in London, 40 cts.; History, Manners, etc., of the Indians, 40 cts.; My Grandmamma Gilbert, 25 cts.; My Grandfather Gregory, 25 cts.; Owen Gladdon's Wanderings, 40 cts.; The Old Sea-Captain, 40 cts.; Homely Hints, 40 cts.; Pleasant Tales, 40 cts.; Country Strolls, 40 cts.; Pithy Papers, 40 cts.; Learning to Think, 35 cts.; Learning to Feel, 35 cts.; Learning to Act, 35 cts.; Learning to Converse, 30 cts.

THE WESLEYAN PSALTER: A Poetical Version of nearly the whole Book of Psalms. By the Rev. Charles Wesley. Versions of some of the Psalms by the Rev. S. Wesley, Sen., the Rev. S. Wesley, Jun., and the Rev. J. Wesley; and Lists of Versions by various Authors. With an Introductory Essay, by Henry Fish, A. M.

The book is both poetically and typographically a perfect gem It is got up as an 18mo., bound in Turkey morocco, full gilt. Price, $2; in gilt muslin, price 50 cts. Also, in 24mo., price 40 cts.

THE HIDDEN LIFE EXEMPLIFIED in the Early Conversion, Pious Life, and Peaceful Death, of Mrs. Florilla A. Cummings. By her Husband. Price 40 cts.

An interesting and edifying biography. The author is President of Holston Female College, Asheville, N. C. His deceased wife was truly an excellent Christian.

THE ART OF PRINTING. Edited by Thomas O. Summers, D.D. 18mo., pp. 185. Price 30 cts.

This volume traces the art preservative of all arts from its rude beginnings to its present approximation to perfection. It has engravings representing presses, etc.

A TREATISE ON SECRET AND SOCIAL PRAYER. By Richard Treffry. 18mo., pp. 215. Price 35 cts.

A very serviceable book.

METHODISM; or, Christianity in Earnest.

SABBATH-SCHOOL OFFERING; or, True Stories and Poems.

THE DAY-SPRING; or, Light to them that sit in Darkness.

The foregoing three volumes are interesting little books, from the pen of Mrs. M. Martin, of South Carolina. They are composed of Sketches, Incidents, Poems, etc., beautifully illustrated and neatly printed. Price, respectively, 30, 30, and 25 cts.

JERUSALEM, ANCIENT AND MODERN. Two vols. Price 60 cts.

Excellent books, embellished with elegant steel engravings.

THE PALM TRIBES—LIFE OF CYRUS—LIFE OF SIR ISAAC NEWTON—SWITZERLAND—IONA—MONEY—THE INQUISITION.

These volumes belong to a series of nearly uniform size, written by some of the first pens of the age. In every one of them a vast amount of useful information is presented in a short compass. They are of that class desiderated by Dr. Arnold—"I never wanted articles on religious subjects half so much as articles on common subjects, written with a decidedly religious turn." They are valuable additions to Sunday-school and family libraries, with special reference to which they have been carefully revised by the Editor. They are sold at 30 cts. each. London in the Olden Times, and more than thirty others, belong to this series.

VARIATIONS OF POPERY. By Samuel Edgar, D. D. 8vo., $1.75.

A masterly work.

VOLCANOES. Price 30 cts.

LIFE AND TIMES OF WYCLIFFE. Price 30 cts.

THE LIFE OF THE REV. JOHN W. DE LA FLECHERE Compiled from the Narrative of the Rev. Mr. Wesley; the Biographical Notes of the Rev. Mr. Gilpin; from his own Letters, and other authentic Documents, many of which were never before published. By Joseph Benson. Price 65 cts.

THE LIFE OF MRS. MARY FLETCHER, Consort and Relict of Rev. John Fletcher, Vicar of Madeley, Salop. Compiled from her Journal, and other authentic Documents. By Henry Moore. Price 70 cts.

Cheap and convenient editions of these two Methodist classics.

STORIES FOR VILLAGE LADS. By the Author of "Stories of Schoolboys," "Frank Harrison," etc. Price 35 cts.

STORIES OF SCHOOLBOYS. By the Author of "Stories for Village Lads." Price 30 cts.

These "lads" and "boys" are English; but we can find a great many like them in the United States, though one seldom meets with such capital stories as these *for* them and *of* them.

ST. PETER'S CHAIN OF CHRISTIAN VIRTUES. By the Rev. C. D. Oliver, of the Alabama Conference. Price 40 cents.

An edifying treatise, based on 2 Pet. i. 5–7.

CHRISTIAN THEOLOGY: By Adam Clarke, LL.D., F.A.S. Selected from his published and unpublished Writings, and systematically arranged. With a Life of the Author. By Samuel Dunn. Price 75 cts.

A carefully revised edition of this great work.

THE GREAT SUPPER NOT CALVINISTIC; being a Reply to the Rev. Dr. Fairchild's Discourses on the Parable of the Great Supper. By Leroy M. Lee, D.D. Price 50 cts.

There is no mincing the matter in this sturdy volume. Even-handed justice is dealt out to Dr. Fairchild, with his aiders and abettors: and the gospel of the grace of God is triumphantly defended from their Calvinistic imputations.

THE ORIGIN AND PROGRESS OF LANGUAGE. Price 35 cts.

A work of no small research, and of great value.

THE THREE SISTERS: A brief Sketch of the Lives and Death of Ann Eliza, Hester Jane, and Laura Washington, Daughters of the Rev. H. J. Perry, of the Kentucky Conference of the M. E. Church, South, who were burned to death in May, 1854. Price 35 cts.

A tribute of parental affection to the memory of three lovely daughters, who in a tragical manner were hastened from earth to their mansions in heaven.

IMMERSIONISTS AGAINST THE BIBLE; or the Babel Builders confounded, in an Exposition of the Origin, Design, Tactics, and Progress of the New Version Movement of Campbellites and other Baptists. By the Rev. N. H. Lee, of the Louisville Conference. Price 40 cts.

The author has performed a needed but disagreeable work; he has done it in a candid, charitable spirit; and we are mistaken if his exposure of the rampant sectarianism which is at the head and front of the New Version movement, do not produce a salutary effect. .

SCRIPTURE HELP. Specially designed for Bible-classes and Sunday-schools. Price 50 cts.

An invaluable "help" to biblical students—*multum in parvo.*

JOSEPH BROWN; or, the Young Tennesseean, whose Life was saved by the power of Prayer. An Indian Tale. Price 30 cts.

This beautiful tale was written by a lady of Tennessee. Her hero is still living in this State—a venerable clergyman. The materials of the narrative were gathered from authentic sources.

LIVES OF EMINENT ANGLO-SAXONS; illustrating the Dawn of Christianity and Civilization in Great Britain. 2 vols., 18mo. Price 70 cts.

These two volumes shed a great deal of light on our Anglo-American laws and literature, and are well adapted to inspire the reader with gratitude for the rich inheritance he has received from the generations of the past.

www.ingramcontent.com/pod-product-compliance
Lightning Source LLC
LaVergne TN
LVHW010226110826
845151LV00004B/1204

* 9 7 8 1 4 2 5 5 2 5 8 0 4 *